T0326941

a man with no talents

a man with no talents

Memoirs of a Tokyo Day Laborer

ŌYAMA SHIRŌ

Translated by Edward Fowler

Cornell University Press   *Ithaca & London*

Cornell University Press gratefully acknowledges support from the International Center for Writing and Translation at the University of California, Irvine, which helped in the publication of this book.

San'ya gakeppuchi nikki, by Ōyama Shirō, copyright © 2000 by Ōyama Shirō. All rights reserved. Originally published in Japan by Hankyu Communications Co., Ltd. English translation rights arranged with Hankyu Communications Co., Ltd., through The English Agency (Japan) Ltd.

English translation and Author's Postscript copyright © 2005 by Cornell University

English translation first published 2005 by Cornell University Press
Printed in the United States of America

Library of Congress Cataloging-in-Publication Data
Ōyama, Shirō, 1947–
   [San'ya gakeppuchi nikki. English]
   A man with no talents : memoirs of a Tokyo day laborer / Oyama Shiro ; translated by Edward Fowler.
      p. cm.
   Includes bibliographical references and index.
   ISBN 978-0-8014-4375-6 (cloth : alk. paper)
   1. Day laborers—Japan—Tokyo. 2. Working class—Japan—Tokyo. 3. San'ya (Tokyo, Japan)—Social conditions. I. Title.
   HD5854.2.J3093   2005
   331.7'98'0952135—dc22   2005041418

Cornell University Press strives to use environmentally responsible suppliers and materials to the fullest extent possible in the publishing of its books. Such materials include vegetable-based, low-VOC inks and acid-free papers that are recycled, totally chlorine-free, or partly composed of nonwood fibers. For further information, visit our website at www.cornellpress.cornell.edu.

Cloth printing   10 9 8 7 6 5 4 3

To Jim

contents

note on the text and acknowledgments

I follow the Japanese custom of writing personal names in the order family name first, given name second. Transliteration of Japanese proper names and terms employs the modified Hepburn system, which uses macrons to indicate most elongated vowels, except in the case of words familiar to the English reader (for example, *Osaka, sumo*). The value of the Japanese yen at the beginning of the twenty-first century has fluctuated, for the most part, between about 100 and 120 to the U.S. dollar. Metric measurements (e.g., centimeters, kilograms) are followed in parentheses by their approximate equivalents in feet and pounds.

I thank the author, Ōyama Shirō, for permission to render his book into English. I thank him also for responding so diligently, both through scrupulous correspondence and then several face-to-face meetings, to numerous questions about the text in the later phases of translation. The author has made certain stylistic choices in writing his book, in both the main text and the chapter headings; I have tried to preserve them. In consultation with the author, I have made a few slight deletions and emendations which, though minor, were deemed crucial for the English-speaking reader's understanding. Most interpolations are in the form of notes, but a few have been added to the text.

I also acknowledge the financial support of the Japan Foundation, which provided a timely short-term grant specifically for the purpose of working on the translation; and of the University of California at Irvine's School of Humanities and International Center for Writing and Translation, which provided further funding for research and a partial subvention of publishing costs. I appreciate the consideration of Dr. Maria Toyoda, then of Stanford University's Asia Pacific Research Center. In her capacity as coordinator of the Center for East Asian Studies symposium, she offered me my first chance to introduce portions of the text to a discerning audience—an event that inspired me to translate the entire book.

I owe a special debt of gratitude to the students participating in an experimental course at UC Irvine in which I featured Ōyama's work and which focused my attention on textual details in a way that would not otherwise have been possible. Thanks to Chungmoo Choi, Kojima Kazuo, and Charles McJilton for helping me with some of the specialized terminology that dots the text; to Stephen C. Bondy and Yoji Yamaguchi for reading the translation in draft and providing equal amounts of encouragement and useful comments; and to Edward Seidensticker—my longtime mentor whose work on Tokyo is one of the chief inspirations for my own involvement with the Low City, and ultimately with San'ya—for his usual incisive remarks on a late draft.

To Ann Sherif, who painstakingly compared the entire manuscript with the Japanese text early on and offered invaluable criticisms, I owe an enormous debt of gratitude. And while credit for countless improvements must go to her and

note on the text and acknowledgments

the others who aided in the process of translation, I alone assume responsibility for any mistakes that remain. Special thanks go to Margaret Mitsutani for her constant encouragement over the years and for first alerting me to this book's existence shortly after it was published. Finally, to James A. Fujii, stimulating colleague and generous friend, to whom I owe far, far more than this book's dedication, thanks for actually buying me a copy and prompting me to read it.

E. F.

Irvine, California

translator's introduction

A Man with No Talents (*San'ya gakeppuchi nikki;* more literally, Living on the brink in San'ya) was first published in 2000. In an afterword to the Japanese edition, Ōyama Shirō explains that he submitted his manuscript to a literary prize screening committee as a lark, feeling not unlike he did when placing an occasional off-track bet on the horses, or as others might feel when purchasing a lottery ticket. The odds of holding the winning ticket were small—indeed, infinitesimal—but they were not nil. Until the winner had been announced, he was as much in the running as anyone else.

His astonishment at learning that his manuscript had actually won the top prize quickly turned into dismay, however; it was the slimness of the odds, after all, that had allowed him to chronicle so uninhibitedly what was, by any ordinary measure, a decidedly unattractive career. San'ya, by far the city's largest *yoseba* (day laborer quarter) and the only one with lodging, had been Ōyama's home for twelve years when he took up his pen and began writing about his life as a resident of Tokyo's most notorious neighborhood. After graduating from university, Ōyama had entered the corporate world and appeared destined to walk down the same path strode by many a white-collar worker, known in Japan as a "salaryman." A singular temperament and a deep loathing of conformity, however, dramatically altered his career trajectory. Ōyama left his job and moved to Osaka's Kamagasaki district, the largest *yoseba* in Japan, and lived there for three years. Later he returned to the corporate world, but fell out of it again, this time for good. After spending a short time on the streets around Shinjuku, home to Tokyo's busiest commuting terminus and a bustling entertainment district, he moved to San'ya in 1987, at the age of forty.

Ōyama's "descent" into a career as a day laborer need not be recounted here; the author addresses the matter himself in the very first chapter, as much as his reticence about personal history will allow. (San'ya residents, having typically cut ties with their families, are usually tight-lipped about their domestic and professional histories; Ōyama is no exception.) He is quick to acknowledge his eccentricity and his inability to adapt to corporate life. Spectacularly unsuccessful as a salaryman yet uncomfortable in his new surroundings, he portrays himself as an outsider, not only vis-à-vis mainstream society but also in relation to his adopted home. It is precisely this outsider's perspective, at once dispassionate yet deeply engaged, however, that made critics in the mainstream press sit up and take note. With his middle-class background and his obvious erudition, the author seemed too far removed from the stereotypical image of the day laborer and too much like themselves to ignore.

These facts go a long way in explaining why a writer with so undistinguished a calling came to receive such a prestigious literary award as the Kaikō Takeshi Prize. Much has been written over the years about San'ya and the institution of casual labor in Japan by print journalists and social scientists, as well as by activists who lived in San'ya—members of a generation preceding the current group of local union leaders which Ōyama writes about in chapter 5. Yet few accounts rise above the merely descriptive, pedantic, or programmatic, and fewer still offer the penetrating sensibility and the fine eye for detail that distinguish this book. Ōyama does not provide the first or most comprehensive overview of the *yoseba* that dot Japan's major cities (see the Suggested Readings at the end of the translation for a sample of writings in English on the subject), but his richly textured narrative of life in the lodging district and at the work site, and above all his compelling portraits of fellow workers, have no equal. The combination of measured self-examination and truly memorable character depictions allows the reader to glimpse a world of which very few Japanese, let alone foreigners, are even aware.

Also highly unusual in the subgenre of writings about San'ya (and perhaps to be found only in the plentiful but obscure anthologies of some remarkably accomplished haiku poets working as day laborers) are Ōyama's philosophical reflections, particularly in the opening and closing chapters. These musings have inspired critics to compare this book with *Hōjōki* (An account of my square hut), a gem of a memoir by the celebrated medieval poet-priest Kamo no Chōmei, who lived out his later years as a recluse but had enormous difficulty forgetting the world he left behind. (It is in this context that one can appreciate Ōyama's obvious passion for politics, not to mention his staunch libertarianism, despite his withdrawal from mainstream society.) Other titles—having nothing to do with Japan—also come to mind for comparison, from Dostoyevsky's *Notes from Underground* to Orwell's *Down and Out in Paris and London*. More than anything, however, Ōyama's book reminds us how distinct an individual writer's view of his environment can be, and how dangerous it is to succumb to the temptation to typecast even a locale like San'ya, the very name of which calls forth all manner of stereotypes for the Japanese public.

This is another way of saying that Ōyama should *not* stand in for the whole of the day laborer community. He himself is quick to caution his readers about the peculiarity, the downright eccentricity, of his habits and opinions. Certainly not all day laborers share Ōyama's prejudices, moreover, about Koreans or foreign migrant workers or Christian missionaries working in San'ya. Indeed, the day laborer union that Ōyama features in chapter 5 has actively collaborated with one Christian church. It has also championed the rights of Koreans, who suffered oppression in Japan across the twentieth century, as well as the rights of foreigners who have migrated to Japan in droves, most of them illegally, in order to meet the demand for the many menial jobs that the Japanese themselves are no longer willing to perform.

That said, thanks to Ōyama's frank and vivid narrative, one cannot simply dismiss the day laborer as unintelligible Other, for it is all too easy to identify with this author's predicament. Readers are likely to be occupying more spacious quarters, with fewer people in the room, than Ōyama, but surely at some time in their lives most of them have dealt with the kinds of anxieties and disappointments that plagued the author and have thought similar thoughts about their roommates, their employers, their peers, and themselves. Like any down-and-out, poverty-ridden day laborer community in Japan—or elsewhere in the world—San'ya is the sort of place about which one is prone to say, "There, but for the grace of God, go I." Ōyama's memoir, however, reminds us that we may well have already set foot in the mindscape evoked by the

author in the pages of this book, and in fact may not have
come back—at least not all the way.

San'ya as a place name has existed from well before the
modern period, but its position in modern history was fixed
by its role as Tokyo's major *yoseba* throughout the second
half of the twentieth century.[1] One of Japan's three principal
yoseba (the others being Kamagasaki, in Osaka, and
Kotobuki-chō, in Yokohama), San'ya became part of a national network of day laborer centers, large and small. These
yoseba were once frequented by perhaps as many as one or
two hundred thousand men—a tiny fraction of the country's
total male workforce, but profoundly important nonetheless
to the success of the postwar economy.

A place of refuge for those who wished to escape the stric-
tures of mainstream society, San'ya, like other *yoseba*, has always been a home for marginalized groups. Here, in addition
to middle-class workers like Ōyama who seem to lack the req-
uisite social skills for functioning in corporate life or who
have simply fallen on hard times, are to be found a variety of
social outcasts. They include career alcoholics and gamblers,
deadbeat dads/husbands, laid-off workers who have bailed
out of the job market, fugitives from creditors or the law, men
with criminal records, the physically and mentally disabled,
and so on. San'ya and other *yoseba* have had a disproportion-
ate number of minority populations as well. The most significant are Koreans, Japan's largest ethnic minority and a vestige
of the colonial period in the first half of the twentieth century

[1] *San'ya* is written with the characters for "mountain" and "valley," but
neither is to be found in this section of Shitamachi or Low City, Tokyo's
older, plebeian district, located mostly east of the Yamanote Loop Line.

when Korea was part of the Japanese empire, and *burakumin*, ethnic Japanese who are descended from premodern outcaste populations. This, too, was only natural; for when all else failed, it was here that work could be had without any questions being asked.

In the chaotic aftermath of World War II, San'ya provided a refuge for vagrants, demobilized soldiers, and returning evacuees without families, all of whom had been relocated by the municipal government from nearby Ueno, a popular amusement district and site of the major terminus for trains arriving from the northern provinces. During the traumatic postwar years, a period of great dislocation, seasonal workers left the villages to find jobs in the city—typically in construction—and often did not return to the farm. With a boost from the Korean War (1950–53), Japan's economy emerged from its postwar doldrums and entered what is known as the "high-growth era" (from the mid-1950s to the early 1970s). This was San'ya's heyday, when some ten to fifteen thousand men occupied the *doyagai* (lodging district) and obtained their jobs off the street or from the two local municipal hiring centers described by Ōyama in stark detail: the Tamahime Employment Agency and, especially, the Welfare Center recruiting office. Thanks in part to these men's labors, the nation's general contractors could maintain a lean payroll even as they completed such monumental projects as the Tokyo Tower and, later, stadiums for the 1964 Olympic Games, the expressway network, and the system of high-speed railways ("bullet trains").

The oil crises of the 1970s and ensuing global recession dampened Japan's economy, however, and day laborer quarters like San'ya began to lose their vigor. Although the economy recovered with a vengeance during the so-called bubble era of the 1980s, day laborers assumed a lesser role. Technological ad-

vances in various industries, including construction, reduced
the need for manual labor; ditches were being dug with machines, not by hand. San'ya's labor pool, which used to be re-
plenished over time by younger and more able-bodied workers,
grew stagnant. The day laborer population itself became
older—as did the nation as a whole—and smaller; it was down
to about five or six thousand at the time of this book's writing.

By the late 1990s, with the end of the postbubble recession
still nowhere in sight, San'ya had become a ghost of its former
self. Demand for the few jobs still available off the street or
from the municipal employment agencies far exceeded the
supply. The younger and the more physically fit were at a distinct advantage. The greatest disadvantage befell those in late
middle age. Having lost their source of income, many men in
their fifties—too old to work but still too young to qualify for
government support—left the tiny single rooms or multi-bed
"bunkhouse" rooms they had once occupied. They either
sought contract work in the provinces, living in barracks
under the poorest of conditions, or took to the streets.

Homelessness—in the sense of not having a roof over one's
head—had once been a rarity in San'ya apart from the small
but very visible population of serious drunks. Now it was
rampant. (Tokyo's overall homeless population, many of
whom live near the banks of the Sumida River in the "blue-
tarp shacks" described by Ōyama, is officially estimated at
something over three thousand, although it may in fact be
closer to double that number. That is only a fraction of the
number of homeless people in New York; yet it is a historic
high for a city that has not seen such a large street population
since the immediate postwar years.) Only the oldest men—
those over sixty-five—had by virtue of age the luxury of quali-
fying for government support, which provided just enough

money to cover lodging and food. The problem, of course, was surviving until that ripe age. (The average life span of the San'ya day laborer is now somewhere between fifty-five and sixty years.) San'ya had turned from an energetic working-class neighborhood into a sleepy welfare town.

This, in short, is the background against which *A Man with No Talents* was written. Ōyama notes in his afterword that lack of work was a blessing of sorts, making it possible for him to devote the several months required to complete his manuscript. (He lived off savings accumulated during the bubble years.) He was totally unprepared, however, for its appearance in print, he confesses, and was fearful of its reception. "If I may disclose a secret hope," he concludes, "it would be that this record of my life be read with only the slightest and mildest of interest, and then be forgotten as quickly as possible."

It would be easy to accuse the author of disingenuousness; he did sign off, after all, on a publishing contract. Yet even this apparent exercise in false modesty has the ring of truth. Exposure to public scrutiny would be anathema to someone like Ōyama, for whom anonymity—which has freed him from all social bonds and allowed him to live and work unimpeded—is so clearly a sustaining force. Although he has indeed offered us an unforgettable record of his life in San'ya, he did so without intending to incite, or sate, curiosity about the man behind the book. Thus, reporters hoping to catch a glimpse of the reclusive author who had burst into the consciousness of the literary world were disappointed when they gathered at the award ceremony for the Kaikō Takeshi Prize. Every bit as suspicious of celebrity as he is of all the varieties of hypocrisy he derides in the pages of his book, and remaining to the end very much in character, Ōyama elected not to attend the ceremony in person and claim his due.

chapter 1

I Become a Bunkhouse
Resident in the San'ya *Doyagai*

BEFORE coming to San'ya I worked for a brief period in Kamagasaki (located in Osaka's Nishinari Ward), where I first cut my teeth as a day laborer. This was when I was between the ages of thirty and thirty-three.

Kamagasaki, too, is a *yoseba*, where day laborers get work off the street, and yet it is as different from San'ya as iron is from lead. The very look of the place, not to mention the character of the people who gather there, contrasts starkly with San'ya. I'm talking about an experience that goes back a good twenty years, but memories of my "Kamagasaki period," and the feel of the quarter and its people, are vividly etched in my mind.

In those days, anyone who alighted from the train at Shin-Imamiya Station, on the Osaka Loop Line, could tell immediately that this was no ordinary neighborhood. A most bizarre-looking landscape, clearly set off from the rest of the city, stretched before one's eyes. Lodging houses of every type (officially termed "simple accommodations," but known to everyone as *doya*) were concentrated in a single area; the only other buildings to be found were those housing the various

1

shops that catered to the needs of doya residents.[1] In the entire quarter there wasn't an apartment or condominium, let alone a house, where a ward office employee or a worker with a desk job at, say, a cement factory, might raise a family. (It is possible, of course, that the offspring of doya managers and shopkeepers might work at said ward office or cement factory.)

The quarter was what might be described as a kind of "liberated zone," where permissiveness, vulgarity, and violence reigned. Visitors to Kamagasaki approaching the area for the first time were thoroughly taken aback by its peculiar inhabitants, so different were they in their dress, their appearance— their very language—from ordinary citizens. This was so even in the middle of the day, when most men were out on the job. At night, the streets of Kamagasaki were as lively as any country fair. For the intrepid day laborer blessed with strength and a skill and brimming with appetites and verve, the Kamagasaki of twenty years ago was a most amusing and stimulating place. Laborers and the police frequently engaged in large-scale clashes. Kamagasaki was not yet the powerless and forlorn town that it has become today, where people await the surrounding community's charity and goodwill. On the contrary, this rowdy, otherworldly "liberated zone" positively intimidated the surrounding community.

I came up to Tokyo at the age of thirty-three, and after trying this and that job without success, I first paid a visit to San'ya in the sixty-second year of the Showa emperor's reign (which is to say 1987)[2] with designs on reactivating my career as a day laborer there. I was now forty years old. "Can you tell me where San'ya is?" I asked a station attendant upon arriving at Minami Senju Station on the Jōban Line, and headed in the direction I was told; yet I never seemed actually to arrive. So I asked the same question of a man walking along the street who looked like a day laborer, and he answered, "This *is* San'ya. You're here!" I looked around, but for the life of me I couldn't see a "liberated zone" anywhere. I approached a police box and inquired, "Is this San'ya?" and got a nod for a reply.

In short, San'ya simply did not exist in the same sense that Kamagasaki did. The latter was an offbeat "liberated zone," clearly segregated, physically and materially, from the living space of ordinary citizens. San'ya, on the other hand, was nothing more than an abstract noun standing for a kind of spectacle in the middle of Tokyo's old Low City. Unlike their Kamagasaki counterparts, moreover, who lived entirely apart from the world around them, the men living in San'ya did not appear to be aliens from another world bent on intimidating ordinary citizens. Indeed, they looked to be none other than the suitless, single male laborers working in construction or in civil engineering projects that they in fact were.

I can't say that a feeling of disappointment didn't well up in me at first, but with time I found that life in San'ya actually suited me better than life in Kamagasaki. That is because I realized I wasn't the kind of person who possessed the physical strength or mental fortitude to enjoy the relentless freedom being offered on a daily basis by Kamagasaki's otherworldly festival—just your average loser who could never stick with a full-time job. I was old enough now for that fact finally to have sunk in.

The demise of my career as a salaryman followed a distinct pattern. The troubles invariably began with my habit of driving myself to extremes in order to conform to professional life (that is, life as a company employee). This excessive compulsion to conform at the outset of my employment had to do no doubt with the deep-rooted fear I have of the collective, which compels its members to join in and work with other people. In order to rid myself of this profound terror of group life and the concomitant urge to escape it, I would will myself at the beginning to adapt to it at all costs. But there is no way to continue the impossible; and indeed, my excessive compulsion to conform would lose momentum over time. A sudden and unmitigated desire to absent myself from work would be accompanied by some psychosomatic disorder, which made me feel physically out of sorts. Even though I realized that this was a compensatory reaction to my original compulsion, I still couldn't prevent the same compulsion from welling up again when I started a new job. Inevitably the cycle would repeat itself: my compulsion toward conformity would eventually break down, after a period of anywhere from three months to a couple of years.

After going through this process countless times, I concluded to myself upon arriving, finally, in San'ya, "I might as well face it: I'm just not suited for human life." Later I read a book or two on psychiatry and determined that my symptoms were akin to a mild form of depression; this very recognition led me to an acceptance that brought with it a sense of liberation. In other words, I think I was able to put behind me, and rather easily, too, what was by any objective measure an utterly failed existence. Thanks to this newfound acceptance, I was finally able to reach an accommodation with myself, even though I couldn't hold down a steady job or get married and was approaching middle age. Yet perhaps, it can also be said, I so lacked any energy for life that I was unable to confront my own sense of failure head on. Wasn't this "acceptance," then, simply a kind of defense mechanism, rooted in human weakness, that allows people in my position to escape the

4

frustration and anxiety and despondency that naturally assail
them?

Merely to embrace such anxiety and frustration requires
some energy and strength. Indeed, simply being tormented by
failure requires a modicum of energy. Deeply cognizant of my
own utter lack of willpower, I strove to distance myself from
what were for me mere extravagances: namely, the just-
mentioned feelings of frustration, anxiety, despondency, and
failure. I was doubtless making the emotional adjustments
necessary to prevent any of these perilous feelings from getting under my skin. Deeply sublimated, they at times still
made their presence known in the form of a disorder in my
autonomic nervous system; but this, I decided, was the unavoidable price I must pay for making those adjustments.
Once I had arrived in San'ya, I instinctively recognized in it
the perfect hiding place—far more so than Kamagasaki, at
any rate—a place where someone lacking any vitality whatsoever could go about the business of accommodating his own
fecklessness and ill luck.

June 1987: San'ya was nothing more than a featureless if
rather squalid and grimy corner of Tokyo's Low City.

In Kamagasaki many doya had only one-mat rooms for individual tenants. Each room had a door with a lock. Imagine
entering a room the size of a single tatami mat. Its ceiling is
just high enough to allow you to stand; there is no window. It
is a completely closed-off space. A floor the size of a single
mat and the ceiling just higher than your head: the quarters
weren't what you'd call roomy; but neither did they seem all
that cramped to me. Stretch yourself out on a tatami and
you'll see what I mean: a single mat is actually wide enough to

feel rather spacious. Someone, say, taller than about 190 cm (6 ft. 3 in.) may feel the room to be too shallow, but being only 165 cm (5 ft. 5 in.) myself, I had absolutely no problem with the length. There was more than enough room to accommodate my outstretched limbs even with my various belongings about me.

San'ya, however, had no single-mat rooms, and so I decided to stay in one of those "simple accommodations" called bunkhouses, which put up eight people per room, each room with four double bunks. Space was not a problem, but having to look at six or seven strangers day and night in the same room—and having to be seen by them—proved to be one; after three weeks at that first bunkhouse, I couldn't stand it any longer and got out.

When I heard about another doya where the bunks were enclosed by curtains that blocked the occupants' view of each other, I located it and moved in. Each bunk also had a television set, I discovered (something unavailable in the one-mat rooms of Kamagasaki), and a good-sized locker with a key. The latter was most convenient, for it meant that I had one mat of space entirely to myself without it being cluttered up with odds and ends. If anything, it felt too spacious. When I lay down on the upper bunk, my belongings in the locker and a curtain to partition me from the outside, the enclosed space—as long and as wide as a tatami and as high as I was tall—actually gave the impression of vastness. A cubicle measuring 1.8 meters long, 1 meter wide, and 1.7 meters high (6 ft. × 3.3 ft. × 5.7 ft.) is indeed quite sizable. I had no quarrel with the dimensions. The problems lay elsewhere.

First, there was the matter of privacy. I took steps to avoid having to look at the other men in the room (as well as avoid their gazes) by putting up pieces of cardboard and thereby sealing my space off even more from the outside. With only a curtain with which to separate myself from the rest of the room, I could see right through it when the light was on— which meant, of course, that I myself could be seen from the other side. The material was not particularly thin, but I could still see my neighbor's every movement through it when it was dark on my side. And so I backed my curtain with cardboard.

Nothing more could be done about the problem, really, than that.

Then there was the matter of noise, and of odors. The odors did not bother me all that much. It would smell when people farted, but that didn't happen very often, and the odor faded away soon enough.

Sometimes a neighbor would return from work with feet that smelled up the entire room. Other times, however, I was the one at fault. No one in particular was to blame. I could tolerate stinking feet well enough. I, too, have my limits, but the smell of someone's odoriferous feet at the end of a hard day of work is simply not that offensive to me. Nor is the smell of food that someone has gamely tried cooking for himself.

The bunkhouse I moved into is at the bottom rung of San'ya's lodging houses in terms of price and one of several in the area officially approved by the welfare office of the city ward I reside in. During the longer holidays, such as New Year's and Obon,³ street people would be put up gratis in a doya like mine for a few days. This is when the odor problem truly got out of hand.

I have found that human body odor reaches its first peak about a week to ten days after a person's last bath. It depends on the season, of course. To go without bathing means going without changing one's clothes, and so you really can't tell whether the odor comes from the body itself or from the garments. At any rate, with this first peak the smell attains the level not merely of a foul odor but of a powerful stench. It doesn't simply waft toward you; it pierces you to the quick. In chemical terms, it is an *organic* stench, of the sort given off by animals.

In its initial stage, however, this piercing, organic stench has a limited range. You aren't even aware of it unless you get right up close. I'm not sure how long it takes for this organic stench to turn into something drier but far more pervasive— an inorganic, wafting odor—but the transformation seems to take place about a month or so after the person in question has stopped bathing.

The aforementioned piercing, organic stench, which materializes in a week to ten days, not only has a limited range but also tends to dissipate once it has attacked the olfactory sense. The "wafting odor" that kicks in after a month's time, on the other hand, is both pervasive *and* persistent. It never seems to let up.

The body odor of street people who slept in the bunk next to me or below me during the long holidays was unmistakably of the "wafting" variety that was a month in the making. It originated in the men's bodies, to be sure, but its center of gravity, so to speak, had shifted to their garments, with the result that bathing did nothing whatsoever to relieve the smell.

I waited in hopes that one of my roommates would voice a complaint; but no such luck. Everyone seemed to be putting up with the odor in silence, and so I, too, had to endure it along with the rest.

When a man goes without bathing for several months on end, his body odor apparently takes on a more definitively inorganic character, until finally it has been transformed into something that is neither foul odor nor stench. True, a strong, persistent smell remains, but it has transcended all stages of foulness. No longer does it resemble the odor emitted by an animal; rather, it has turned into something more value neutral, such as the odor of a rotten tree, or mud, or metal ore. This is what I am told, although I haven't been able to verify it myself.

By far the most difficult thing to cope with when living in a bunkhouse is the noise, especially the sound of the human voice. Occupying a bed totally exposed to the gaze of your bunkmates encourages you to lower your voice and otherwise limit the amount of noise you make. When your line of sight is blocked by a curtain or by a piece of cardboard, however, you become less sensitive. The reality of seven or eight men crammed together in a single room no longer enters your consciousness. The fact that it doesn't is the reason, of course, why it is even possible to lead a normal, peaceful life in such a place for years on end. Yet that very lack of awareness becomes at times the source of trouble.

Snoring is potentially the biggest nuisance of all, I suppose, but fortunately I've never had to confront the problem close up. I have been bunkmates with some men who were in the habit of snoring when they drank too much, but luckily none of them stayed in the doya for long.

Be that as it may, one lives in a bunkhouse with the understanding that any noise will be picked up by one's neighbor. Farting and burping, turning the pages of a newspaper or a book, the rustling of clothes when turning over in one's sleep, switching channels on the television (the TV has no remote), pulling the tab on a can of coffee or other beverage, chewing food and gulping a drink . . . whatever noise I made my bunkmates would hear, and whatever noise they made I would be forced to listen to. After a while, therefore, these various sounds would go unnoticed and just become part of living. As long as people are alive and moving about, it is impossible for them not to make sounds such as these. There was no one who stayed in my room so dull witted as not to realize this.

Noise gets to be a problem when it becomes mixed up with a man's sense of pride, however, as in the following example.

When getting out of bed (or getting down from bed, if sleeping in an upper bunk), and when getting back in (or climbing back up), we have to draw the curtain across our bunks; and when we do, the curtain makes a sharp, scraping noise on its rail. Most men will try to temper the noise by opening and closing the curtain with a gentle, sliding motion. About one man in ten, however, will fling the curtain open or shut as though his reputation were on the line. Over time he comes to relish the sound; eventually he starts making far more noise than necessary in his other activities as well. You can tell he's watching the rest of us in the room and waiting to see how we'll react.

"So, you can take this much? OK, then how about this?" Whereupon he raises the stakes, carefully weighing his own burgeoning ego against the response of his bunkmates to the increased noise level. This is how he operates, scrupulously ascertaining the risk posed by the other men all the while.

The rest of us go on putting up with the man's game of dare until someone finally lodges a complaint with the "front desk" (that is, the manager). But what can one say to a man so relentlessly arrogant—someone who stomps, not walks, into the room; who sneezes or farts with an earsplitting sound; who bangs the television when changing channels, all with a noise way out of proportion to the act?

10

Usually, then, we simply wait for such men to depart, quietly enduring their arrogant posturing. Once in a while, however, we get the manager to demand that they change their ways. An indispensable requirement for the would-be San'ya lodging house manager is having the aggressiveness, as well as the commanding presence (backed up by ability to use force), to put such men in their place.

I recall an incident that occurred when a large man who looked to be in his forties happened to be in the bunk next to mine. An extremely quiet person, he was a model of discretion and hardly made a sound even when opening and closing his curtain. This man gave me a tongue-lashing for doing something I hadn't even given a thought to before he arrived. Then he proceeded to whack me on the sole of my foot.

Lights are out at 11:30 in our doya. That night, I didn't want to put down the mystery novel that had absorbed me all evening, and so I opened the little window next to my bunk and continued reading by the hallway light. It was already about 1:00 a.m., and I was determined to read on until dawn if necessary. I noticed that the ordinarily quiet man in the bed next to me was mumbling to himself, but I had no idea that his words had any relation to my actions.

As I continued to read, my neighbor's mumbling assumed an angry tone; yet I still had no idea that it was directed at me. A while later, he muttered, "Cut out the noise, bastard!" I stopped reading when I heard him get out of his bunk. He pulled open my bunk curtain, poked his head in near my feet, and yelled, "Quiet in there!" At the same time, he gave the sole of my right foot two blows with his fist.

By the time I rose up in astonishment, the man had already withdrawn from the foot of my bed and was on his way (I think) to the toilet. The sound of my turning the pages of my mystery novel had grated on his nerves. I'd been totally oblivious to the effect it had on him.

I made some sort of apology to the man upon his return, but got only a "Shut up!" in reply. He had been staying at the doya for less than a week at the time of the incident. He was a mild-mannered, contemplative man with whom I had not had an actual conversation but to whom I was quite favorably disposed. I never imagined him to be the high-strung type. When all is said and done, one can never be too quiet in a doya; it is definitely possible, however, not to be quiet enough even when one is trying his best to be so, as I found out.

I recall another roommate who previously occupied the bunk of the man who hit me on the sole of my foot. A frail-looking man of at least sixty years, he had a very distinctive walk, with the short, unsteady steps of a toddler.

This man made an incessant clicking noise with his tongue when lying down in his bunk and listening, I think, to the TV with his earphone. Out the sounds would come, at regular intervals: a soft "che, che," or a "chi, chi." On some days he made no sound at all. It was a rare day, in fact, that he did click his tongue; but on such days he would keep it up with the same steady rhythm for hours on end. It did not appear that there was anything in his line of vision (such as whatever he was watching on TV) that was worth clicking his tongue about.

This habit really got on my nerves; in fact, it nearly drove me crazy. There he was just beyond my curtain, his head and his lips a mere two or three feet away from me, clicking his tongue continuously. Maybe he had some pent-up grievance to which he gave voice through his tongue clicking. If so, then

chapter 1

I would have to interpret his act as something akin to an involuntary physiological response, like a hiccup or a yawn.

You can't carp at a person's tics. The problem may not have been purely involuntary, but it was obviously something similar to that. It wasn't really a matter I could complain about to the front desk.

Despite my reasoning, the man's clicking noises did not cease to assault my ears or grate on my nerves. One day I accosted him directly.

All to no avail. My kind of protest, delivered in the form of a lament, had no effect in a place like San'ya. I must have realized, however dimly, that complaints lodged here had to take the form of threats if they were to have any impact. Yet even after all these years, I still hadn't nurtured the ability to intimidate people. It was a lost cause.

This is how the man responded to my complaint: "I don't think I was doing anything that requires a lecture from you, but maybe I was, if you say so. I'm really sorry. OK, I'll be careful from now on. If it happens unconsciously, though, you'll have to let me know each time. Anyway, I'm really sorry about it."

I could hardly inform him of his habit on each and every occasion, however. I didn't know if his words were truly sincere or merely a conscious and crafty means of evading the issue. The tongue clicking did not stop after my complaint. I cautioned him a couple of times subsequently in the same manner as before, with no success. The days of being tormented by his tongue clicking continued. I would defend myself by transferring the TV earphone to the ear that picked up the sound, turning up the volume on the set, and stuffing the other ear with an earplug.

I was certainly the closest one in the room to his bunk. Soft though the sound might have been, however, I couldn't believe that it reached my ears only. Yet it seems that no one besides me registered a complaint. What did this mean? Was I the lone occupant with hypersensitive nerves? Was it possible for a person to be more tolerant than others of smelly feet and yet far less so of tongue clicking? Was any normal person simply oblivious to a continuous, persistent clicking sound emitted from a place about eighty centimeters from his ears? The sound didn't go away completely even when I turned up the volume on the TV set and stuffed an earplug into the other ear, but I couldn't bring myself to complain further. This man, too, finally left after a time.

My room has seven occupants. (The eighth bunk is used for storage.) Four bunks are occupied by regulars, the other three by transients who come and go every few days or weeks or months. The attendant at the front desk brings in a newcomer as I am lying in my bunk. "You're in room ———, bunk number ———. Please remember it."

The attendant leaves, and I can hear the sound of the newcomer placing his belongings on the bunk, opening a window, turning on the fluorescent lamp. Later, the sound of him laying out his futon, removing garments from his bag and hanging them up, and lifting the tab on a can of some beverage. You can't tell exactly what makes a man tick from just these few sounds. Nor can you tell even after two or three days have gone by and the sounds made by the unseen newcomer increase in variety and number. But you can certainly grasp the essential things.

Is he someone who tramps loudly as he walks down the corridor? How does he open and close his curtain? What sort of pushing noise does he make when changing the channels?

Or slurping noise, when he drinks? Listening to these various sounds, you can pretty well figure out the degree of forbearance necessary in dealing with a particular bunkmate, even without laying eyes on the man or hearing him talk. And until we regulars (myself included) do figure it out, we are on tenterhooks for a day or two, lying in our bunks with bated breath and our ears tuned to the newcomer's every movement.

I have lived in this same bunkhouse for most of my career in San'ya, sharing a room with six others and separated from them by a single curtain. The manager who sat at the front desk when I moved in has already departed this world, having succumbed to liver cancer. I suppose I can number myself among the old-timers at this doya.

I can't say that life here has been all that comfortable, but I've made an effort to develop something resembling affection for the destiny that has landed me in this place. This is how I look at it: What would have happened if by some mistake I'd remained stuck in a job with an ordinary firm? Unable to resist the all the static around me, I probably would have gotten married and had a family. Yet would such a life course really have been better than my life here in a doya? I think not. I doubt very much that I could have maintained my mental equilibrium had I been placed in those circumstances.

I am a vessel that was made to hold nothing more than my own body and soul. I have been quite incapable of shouldering any other burden than these. My psyche would have been crushed by any added weight. The consequence would have been not just my mental breakdown and a life of confinement but also the certain misfortune visited on family members as a result of my breakdown. At the very least, then, I've been able to prevent myself from becoming the source of other people's unhappiness. Those who are made like me or who have turned out like me would surely have ended up leading the kind of life I'm leading in the sort of place I'm living in, regardless of the era. Yet might I not take secret pride in the fact that I have been able to limit the misfortune I've caused others to the bare minimum? (In the case of my parents it really can't be helped.) This is how I sometimes view things. At other times, when I'm in a more positive mood, I fancy that I have happened upon a life here that quite agrees with me. There is nothing to add or detract, and I really have no cause for dissatisfaction.

I have always tried to steer my thoughts in this direction. I intend to stay the course. If possible, I'd like to remain lost in these thoughts and slide as if in a trance toward death. For someone like me, who is on the threshold of old age, such a wish is akin to a prayer of supplication.

No matter what the future holds, I am determined not to harbor any bitterness toward the fate that has led me to this place.

chapter 2

A Generation or So Ago
I Would Never Have Made
It as a Day Laborer

MY LIFE as a day laborer in Tokyo, which began in Showa 62 (1987), can be divided fairly evenly into two six-year periods before and after the collapse of Japan's so-called bubble economy. Looking back, I can say that the first six-year period, during the bubble era, was a golden age for us day laborers—just as it must have been for real-estate speculators.

In those days, it simply wasn't possible to step out of my doya in the morning with the intention of finding work and not come away with a job. Indeed, I'd be hailed by several agents who recruited workers off the street on my way to the main drag around Namidabashi intersection, where most of the recruiting takes place. After two or three months in San'ya, I stopped getting my work off the street and began requesting jobs through the San'ya Welfare Center recruiting office,[1] which meant that I had to wave off all the street agents on my way to the Center. You could tell right away from their rough manner that they were not the sort who meekly took no for an answer, so turning them down required a certain knack.

At 6:30 a.m., when the shutters of the recruiting office

slowly began to rise, we would crouch down and crawl underneath, trot toward the bank of windows (all of which had signboards posting several jobs), and begin examining the particulars of each job. We'd shuttle back and forth from window to window, studying the signboards all the while. Once we'd made up our minds, we would step up to the proper window, present our registration cards (issued by the recruiting office), and call out the number of the job we wanted to the clerk: "Number seven!" "Number twenty-two!" and so on.

The signboards at each of the seven windows could post up to five job listings, for a total of thirty-five listings at any one time; but in those days there were too many jobs to post at once. When someone picked a job and the light next to it went out, another listing would take its place and the light would turn right back on again. Some of the more preferable jobs would be posted later on, so we knew better than to jump at one of the first thirty-five jobs unthinkingly. The recruiting office clerks, meanwhile, anticipating that there would be no takers for the less appealing jobs, would try sticking some of them in here and there among the first thirty-five without attracting notice. They couldn't use the same tactic every day, however, or they'd run the risk of not filling their initial job openings, so I imagine that they had headaches of their own.

During the bubble era's summer months (when people didn't want to work because of the heat), maybe 20 or 30 percent of the offerings went untaken. The light next to some postings on the signboard would remain lit as late as 7:00 or even 8:00 a.m.

Even after the stock-market crash in the early 1990s, there was no dramatic decline in the number of job listings. That number did not go down, I'm fairly certain, until a year or two after the bubble economy had collapsed. The landscape of San'ya in the morning was transformed, however, once the country entered the Heisei recession in the bubble era's aftermath. The number of street agents visibly declined, and the ones who remained no longer hailed us as they had done before. This time it was the other way around: whenever an agent appeared before us, we day laborers would approach him and ask whether there was work, only to be waved off as if we were in their way. The agents working the street were there only to assign job locations to the laborers with whom they already had a nodding acquaintance.

It was then that the atmosphere at the Center recruiting office also underwent a complete change.

In order to secure a spot in front of the shutters, men began climbing right over the seven-foot high slatted iron fence surrounding that corner of the building, paying no heed to the locked gate. All it took was one man, of course, and then everyone who wanted a job from the Center was forced to do the same thing. The next thing you knew, men were getting up at around 4:00 a.m., climbing over the fence, and putting down paper bags and such to secure their places in line in front of the shutters. The hour got earlier and earlier: four o'clock became two o'clock, and two o'clock became one. In the end, the men were scaling the fence the previous evening and putting down their bags to mark their spots. The Center soon caught wind of this and tried to put a stop to it. That didn't happen right away, but then one official told the laborers, "Anybody going over the fence doesn't get a job here." And just like that, the climbing came to a halt. No one was able to stake out a place in front of the shutters until Center officials arrived at 6:00 a.m. and opened the gate.

Four shutters separated us from the recruiting office windows and their job listings; we waited until 6:00 a.m. for the gate to open and let us in as far as those shutters. Now the struggle for position focused on the gate itself and on the men's place in line in front of it. At first, paper sacks and shoulder bags—and as time went on, empty cans—would be placed in a row in front of the black metal gate. The empty cans made their appearance at a progressively earlier hour: 4:00 a.m. became 1:00 a.m.; 1:00 a.m. became 8:00 the previous evening; and finally, 8:00 p.m. became 5:00 p.m., the hour the gate was closed. Disputes about the proper order of these cans were a matter of course.

For example, there was the question of whether the place of someone who simply left his empty can and returned to his doya for the night was worth as much as the place of someone who camped out in front of the gate with his can in order to protect his spot. The unspoken rule that emerged was: Anyone who left his can unattended couldn't complain if it got knocked out of place. The idea eventually caught on: it paid to stay with your can.

At 6:00 a.m. four or five Center officials would arrive at the scene, jangling their keys. They would first rouse the street people sleeping in front of the shutters (these were not job seekers) and make them clear away their gear. Then, after kicking away the empty cans, they approached the line of us who had been maneuvering for position. "How many today?" someone in line might ask. An official would announce the number. On days when job offerings were few, some men would give up right then and there and drop out of line.

On the days I secured a spot in the very first row in front of the black metal gate, I would dig in and wait for the officials to open it, feeling the crushing weight of those behind me at my back. As the gate opened, the thirty to forty (sometimes as many as fifty) job seekers who had been pushing and shoving each other now made a dash for the shutters.

Once in a while a man who'd camped out with his can since, say, 1:00 a.m. would be bumped out of line by a latecomer who arrived at the "regular" commuting hour of 5:00 a.m. In this situation only agility and brute strength counted for anything. If you fell out of line, the five hours spent waiting from 1:00 until 6:00 a.m. when the gate opened were for naught. Moreover, the men farther back in line would sometimes get caught up in the jostling. When one of them tried to support himself by grabbing at the arm or waist of the man ahead of him, the man being grabbed, even if he didn't fall down, might get pushed out of line. I myself have been forced out in this way many times. The man behind me harbored no ill will, and he certainly didn't do it on purpose. I, too, have clutched the arm of the man in front of me, and I did so through blind instinct. Such incidents were simply unavoidable.

This was the routine: Center officials opened the gate; we stampeded through and made a dash for the shutters. The closest ones were about fifteen feet away (that is, the distance from the first row of job seekers in front of the gate to the nearest shutter); the farthest ones some forty feet away (the distance to the farther of two shutters located around a right-angle turn). It was here that not only agility but also the ability to make split-second decisions came in handy.

For example, let's say you were in the fourth row of men waiting in front of the gate. Ordinarily, you'd give up on the two closest shutters and head for the rear shutters around the corner (and that would generally be the right choice). But this time you notice a chance opening in front of the nearby shutter, and you slip right in.

In other words, you had to be aware, even as you headed
for the rear shutters around the corner, that it sometimes behooved you not to make the turn. And that very awareness increased the tension surrounding the sprint through the open
gate. Once we reached the shutters, our places were set and
our order of waiting thus determined. Not surprisingly, that
itself became the basis for the next round of disputes. A total
of twelve lines would form in front of the shutters (three lines
for each of the four shutters). One of the shutters was set off
from the rest by a pillar, and if you got caught up against it
when making your dash, you'd never make it in, even if you
had been in the first row in front of the gate. The four or five
hours spent waiting all night would then be wasted.

A man caught unawares against the pillar would then move
to the right or left and try to squeeze himself into one of the
three lines on either side of him. This meant in effect that four
men would be fighting for the first three spots (that is, the first
row) in front of a shutter. Very rarely, a fistfight would break
out, but usually one of the four men backed down. I was one
of those who always ended up yielding his spot.

The shutters went up at 6:30 a.m., but at an excruciatingly
slow pace. Those who had won one of the dozen coveted
spots in the front row of the four shutters that day would slip
their hands underneath the shutters as soon as the metal was
an inch or two off the ground. When the gap had widened
sufficiently they stuck their heads through and slithered into
the office area. Once inside, they rose to their feet and raced
to the windows. The closest window was about ten or twelve
feet away; the farthest, perhaps twenty-five or thirty.

The men would thrust the registration cards they had
clutched in their right hands through the windows and wave
them in the clerks' faces, shouting any number that came to

mind. The matter of choice no longer entered the picture. They simply foisted their cards on the clerks, ignorant of the job description or wages or location. They found out what kind of job they had gotten only when they received their work sheets—at which point there was no changing things, no matter how hateful the work.

Those who failed to secure a spot in the very front row would be riding on the heels of the men who had already disappeared headfirst into the office. In all, forty or fifty men scrambled into the office in a symphony of strained movement as the shutters slowly rose: the first row of men on their bellies, the next row on their knees, the ones after that in a crouch. By the time they were all inside, the shutters had still not opened all the way. That is how quickly everyone moved through.

The movements were not as violent as what you might expect in, say, a game of rugby (everyone was heading in the same direction, after all), but they were crisper and more rapid, and above all more tension filled. We all had our bruises and scrapes. Once I saw a man's face half covered with blood flowing from a head wound. We usually did not sustain serious injuries when going through this ritual even when getting hammered from all sides, because we kept low to the ground, but this man must have struck his head on one of the shutter's sharp edges.

Occasionally a man caught up against the previously mentioned pillar would approach a shutter from the side and try forcing himself through a space wide enough for only three men. Then he, along with the three others in the front row, would get wedged in, stuck together like dumplings on a stick and making it impossible for any of the four to enter the recruiting office. Everyone in the three columns behind them, caught in the storm, so to speak, would lose out on the competition for a job that day. If you got mixed up in something like this, all you could do was resign yourself to your misfortune. Along with agility and discernment, then, sheer luck was a factor in this competition.

Sometimes I would see men who'd been deprived of their freedom of movement by others riding on their heels lash out at the perpetrators and try to pick a fight. These men were definitely not "shutter regulars." The regulars knew full well that piling on top of others and getting piled up on was simply part of the game, and that it was useless to protest. You never heard complaints from them.

This, in short, is how things were until about a year ago (which is to say, until 1998). As I write (in the fall of 1999), the recession has actually deepened, yet one no longer sees this brutal struggle for survival going on in front of the Center.[2] In the days when dozens of men gathered at the Center gate with bloodshot eyes, there was at least the expectation that, by staying up all night to secure a spot in line, then sprinting to the shutters the next morning and slithering underneath, one could land a job. Now, however, Center regulars entertain no such expectation. Conditions have grown far worse. A very small number of men, intent on getting work, continue to secure spots in front of the gate. Unlike a couple of years ago, however, these men are in the market for long-term jobs at a *hanba*, not for work by the day.[3] The number of men who gather at the Center early in the morning has plummeted, and those who still come cannot get work. Those tension-filled scenes of laborers wriggling underneath the shutters are a thing of the past; it is a much more tranquil affair now. No longer do men storm the place by the dozen in hopes of landing one of the three to five jobs available that day.

24

chapter 2

Many Center regulars have disappeared from the scene altogether. Some simply gave up looking for a job and have made the descent from day laborer to vagabond. In the following chapters I shall write in more detail about these people, as well as about others who continued to make an appearance at the Center—regularly or not.

The early risers who managed to get work for the day at the Center were given stamps by their employers to paste on their "white cards" (that is, unemployment insurance cards). When they had collected 26 stamps over a two-month period (it used to be 28 stamps until a few years ago), they were eligible to receive a stipend of 7,500 yen (up from 6,200) per day on the days they did not work. Thus, by working only about half the month (13 days, down from 14), they were assured of an income of 7,500 yen on the days that they couldn't land a job. This meant that a day laborer, after working just 13 days, could earn somewhat more in a month than a college graduate made in an entry-level position, once you factored in the unemployment dole. I had very little to complain about in the days when I was earning what was hardly an insignificant sum for a single man, and living as I did an almost completely unfettered existence.

The kinds of work to be had through the Center included concrete pouring; pick-and-shovel work (that is, digging and reinforcing holes); assisting a skilled worker, usually a *tobi*[4] (less commonly, a carpenter or ironworker); and, finally, the myriad odd jobs to be had at a construction site. My impression is that, except for the first three job categories (concrete pouring, ditch digging, and tobi's helper), the majority of the jobs were relatively easy work that could be handled even by a woman in her forties or fifties. The work we were assigned was an absolute cinch most of the time, because a good 60 to

25

70 percent of it consisted merely of odd jobs ("miscellaneous work" and cleanup). Indeed, during the bubble years, I almost never took a job that was *not* "miscellaneous work" or cleanup.

There is an ongoing debate about who is the strongest sumo wrestler of all time: Musashimaru or Futabayama.[5] Fans of Musashimaru argue that one need only compare the records held by, say, former champion track-and-field athletes and swimmers during Futabayama's time with those of the current record holders, to arrive at the obvious conclusion. If Futabayama were put in among today's top wrestlers, he would be dwarfed by the competition: he was as light as Terao and shorter to boot.[6] How could he possibly pit himself against the likes of Musashimaru, who stands 190 cm (6 ft. 3 in.) and weighs upward of 235 kg (500 lbs.)? The same could be said for such former sumo greats as Tochigiyama, who weighed less than 90 kg (200 lbs.), and Tamanishiki, who stood barely 170 cm tall (5 ft. 7 in.). Could they succeed even on the amateur circuit nowadays, given that some of the American wrestlers participating in tournaments stand more than 2 meters (6 ft. 7 in.) tall and weigh well over 300 kg (660 lbs.)?[7]

Fans of Futabayama, on the other hand, make their case on the basis of their perception of how strong the average Japanese man living on a farm was before the era of high economic growth. They point out that nearly every youth in those days, short of stature though he may have been, could easily lift a 60-kilo (132-lb.) bale of rice. They go on to argue what a formidable wrestler Futabayama must have been, seeing as how he was the standout among wrestlers of his time,

who were themselves the product of this generation of very
sturdy young men.

Who is right? Obviously, no one can say for sure. For me,
however, there is one telling fact: In the days before the economic boom of the 1950s and 1960s, Japanese men were part
of a social system that demanded far greater physical strength
than is required of today's Japanese.

When I first started out as a day laborer in Kamagasaki
twenty years ago, the weight of a cement bag used at construction sites was already down to 40 kg (88 lbs.). But even a
40–kilo bag was a strain when you had to bend over, wedge
your fingers underneath it, and lift it off the ground with a
grunt. "Wow, that's heavy!" you'd be thinking. Lifting bags
off the top of an eye-level or chest-level pile onto one's shoulder wasn't all that difficult, even for me, but hoisting the last
bag from the bottom of the pile onto my shoulder seemed to
me the toughest job imaginable during my early years as a day
laborer. I was forever moving those 40-kilo cement bags from
one place to another on the construction site, lifting them to
my shoulder or cradling them in my arms. As long as I walked
on level ground, I could go any distance. Sometimes, though, I
had to move the bags upstairs, from the ground floor up two
or three stories. This was grueling work, and I'd take frequent
rests on my way up the stairs, lowering the cement bags onto
the railing where it widened out in the landings between
floors.

I was astounded to learn that these cement bags used to
weigh 50 kg (110 lbs.) up until the Showa thirties (1955–64). I
don't doubt for a moment that I would have been disqualified
as a construction worker back then for that reason alone. Lifting a 50-kilo bag of cement would have been quite beyond my
physical capacity. The standard 40-kilo bag, which my muscles

can just barely control, was replaced just two or three years
ago by a 25-kilo (55-lb.) bag. I remember thinking how light it
felt at first, but now that I've grown accustomed to the weight,
it no longer feels nearly as light as it once did. The fact that a
cement bag used to weigh twice this much is simply beyond
my ability to comprehend. Every time I look at a cement bag, I
thank my lucky stars that this is not the Showa thirties. Digging ditches by hand in the days when almost no heavy equipment (power shovels, bulldozers and the like) was available, or
pouring concrete by hoisting it by the bucketful or wheelbar-
row up to the fifth or sixth floor in lieu of a pump truck—
when I hear about how things were back then, I cannot help
being thankful. Someone as weak as I am could never have
shown his face at a construction site in the Showa thirties.

I actually thought of myself as truly fortunate to have a day
laboring career in the post-high-growth era. A frail person like
me unable to adapt to the collective life never could have
made it in Japan during those years or earlier. I continued to
think I was fortunate even when the collapse of the bubble
economy led to the Heisei recession, at least while it was still
possible to receive an unemployment dole. But no longer; any
such thoughts I once entertained, along with the sense of gratitude that accompanied them, have disappeared entirely.

No longer do I believe that my life, as I face the second
decade of the Heisei era on the threshold of old age, is more
blessed than it would have been were I facing the Showa thirties as a frail old laborer. I think of myself as a man of few appetites who is satisfied with very little, but even I have become
prone to grumbling at the severity of life in San'ya these past
few years. The hope I had embraced during the bubble period—the feeling of "Yes, I can get by"—has disappeared
from my heart without a trace. The golden age in San'ya
appears indeed to be a thing of the past.

28

chapter 3

Tsukamoto-san Disappears

A KIND of fraternal relationship—and the emotions that spring from it—comes into play among the men who gather early in the morning at the Center in hopes of getting work through the recruiting office. And yet these Center regulars, colleagues of a sort though they may indeed be, maintain their distance from each other in a way that is far from genteel. This is what inevitably happens: You go to a construction site with another man from the Center. You spend eight or nine hours in conversation with him. You part company at the work site having learned his name. And then, when you run into the man in front of the Center on some other day and (naturally) pay your respects, you get hardly a glance in return. This happens time and time again. Sometimes you are ignored altogether.

There are some men who might actually say hello to you during those early hours in front of the Center, but they'll look right past you when you greet them on the street elsewhere in the neighborhood. When this first happened to me, I couldn't help thinking to myself, "What a bastard!" After living in San'ya for a few years, however, I realized that I'd fallen into the same habit myself. If you had to acknowledge every single person you'd spent time with at a construction site, you'd be forced to stop and chat each time you walked down the street in San'ya. You really have no choice but to prioritize your relationships; *not* responding to someone's greeting, unseemly though it may appear, is actually one way of doing this.

You can't tell what a man is like until you've spent several hours with him at the work site. The fact that I was ignored on the street in San'ya (that is, regarded as the sort who didn't merit a greeting) by someone I had worked with side by side at a construction site meant, surely, that judgment had already been passed on my behavior and my actions on the job.

I recall an incident that occurred in the middle of summer about five or six years ago, although I can't be sure whether it was right before or after the deepest period of recession. The typical offering at the Center recruiting office then was just one or two jobs; three or more listings in a day was a rarity. On this occasion, however, a single construction site was recruiting seven or eight men to dig ditches and reinforce them with sheet piles. Jobs of this sort were a killer during the summer months. The fact that I took it goes to show just how little work was available then.

When I arrived at the construction site, however, I discovered that there were in fact no ditches to dig. This is the way some companies operate. If a firm posts a listing for odd jobs and cleanup but in fact makes the men do sheet piling or scaffolding or some other high-intensity (that is, demanding) work, day laborers will scream bloody murder because the work doesn't match the job description. If, on the other hand, a firm posts a listing for ditch digging and sheet piling work but actually uses the men for odd jobs and cleanup (paying them at the same rate for any job), nobody utters a peep. As a result, many contractors end up advertising all work they solicit through the Center as ditch digging and sheet piling because it's just too much trouble to ascertain the exact nature of each job needed at their various construction sites. So it's possible for a man to go to a site expecting hard labor and wind up with an easy day of cleanup work. He's not going to complain; indeed, he feels as though he's gotten a break.

Anyway, that's what happened on this particular day. We were told, however, that one man in our group would be needed for some heavy-duty work—not sheet piling, but ditch digging. The other six or seven men would be doing light work indoors while this one man wielded a shovel under a blistering sun—and at the same pay, too. It was the difference between paradise and inferno.

After the morning roll call and instructions, the site manager asked one of us to volunteer to dig ditches. That kind of work in midsummer is a nightmare. You could be stricken with heat prostration and, even if you didn't die from it, still wind up in an ambulance. At the very least, you'd be putting down your shovel every ten minutes to fetch a drink of water, and all that water made you lose your appetite. Nobody willingly took on this kind of job.

Every day laborer there stood silent; not one man raised his hand. All of us stared at the ground, our eyes lowered, hoping that the next man would volunteer. I kept quiet, too, feeling the same way as everyone else. If the site manager had added an extra thousand yen or two to the wages, someone might have stepped forward, but he probably didn't have the authority. The silence grew uncomfortably long. All the manager had to do was assign the job outright to one of us, of course, and the one so ordered would have had to take it; but the

manager would then have had an extremely bitter employee
on his hands.

After a very long while, someone finally volunteered. It was
Kinoshita-san, the oldest member of our seven- or eight-man
group. He was already more than sixty years old at the time, I
think. A slight, slender-shouldered, reticent man, he raised his
hand with obvious reluctance. "All right, damn it, I'll do it."
Everyone else in our group heaved a collective sigh of relief at
these words.

Now this, to me, was an act of gallantry in the truest sense.
Gallantry, I realized—as someone who could never possess it
himself—was stoically taking on a task when it clearly involved a personal sacrifice. Even I, who tended to regard with
suspicion the concept of "love" in the Christian sense of joy-
fully or spontaneously sacrificing oneself (isn't it, after all, a
variation on the lust for power?), could only tip my hat un-
hesitatingly to a man with this quality. Here was an act of
which I was simply incapable.

Kinoshita was a man I often met up with in the front row at
the shutters, someone with whom I engaged in a ritual I secretly termed "bowing toward Mecca." Right before the shutters opened at 6:30 a.m., the Center officials would announce
over their public address system the number of job listings
being offered that day and warn us about the signboards that
were reserved for specialized jobs such as scaffolding work
and the operating of heavy equipment. The shutters opened
up two or three minutes after that, and when they did, those
of us in the very front would prepare to enter by pressing our
foreheads to the concrete floor, placing both hands next to
our ears, and raising our buttocks. This posture closely resembled that of Muslims in an attitude of prayer. No one made
any mention of the fact, but I called this posture "bowing

toward Mecca" and tried to give it currency by introducing
the term to others. It never caught on.

Saying that I "bowed toward Mecca" with someone is the
same as saying that both of us had secured a spot right in
front of the shutters. (Those in the second row or further back
had no need to assume the posture.) Kinoshita, like me, was
one of those who got up at 2:00 or 3:00 a.m. and arrived
early at the Center. That meant we spent several hours together on various occasions waiting for the gate to open up at
6:00; but we had never engaged in any intimate conversations
up to that point. He was, as I said, a man of few words. We
would say hello when we passed each other on the street (he
was someone who *would* return a greeting), but ours was not
a close relationship.

After that manly act of volunteerism, I couldn't help ac-
knowledging his superior humanity, but that didn't bring us
any closer. Two or three years later, Kinoshita stopped showing up at the recruiting office. I asked the other regulars where
he'd gone. No one knew. He kept a very low profile at the
Center.

For the "regulars" who get jobs through the Center, the recruiting office had the feel of a workplace. One obvious difference from a normal workplace, however, was that here a man
who had showed up two or three times a week for years on
end might suddenly disappear and never be heard from again.
No one in San'ya is going to tell you, "This is my last day
here. I won't be coming to the Center any more. Thanks for
everything." You might ask around about someone ("I haven't
seen Mr. So-and-so lately. Do you know what's happened to
him?"), but nobody will know a thing, and after a while all

talk about him stops. This is the way people around here disappear from the scene. I'm one of the old-timers among those getting their work at the Center recruiting office, having come here now for more than ten years. The old-timers I knew at the beginning have nearly all disappeared (in the manner just described), and so almost no one even knows that I'm an old-timer myself.

Tsukamoto-san was one of the very few Center regulars who'd been around longer than I had. His career as a day laborer in San'ya went back much farther than mine (nearly thirty years, I think), but he started getting his work from the Center about thirteen or fourteen years ago, which is to say about a year before I did. For the first six or seven years after Tsukamoto and I started coming to the Center, there was work to be had in abundance. When you found no job to your liking, you had the option of skipping work for the day and picking up unemployment compensation. If you didn't come across anything to your liking the next day, either, you simply took whatever was available then, like it or not.

Regardless of how familiar someone's face has become in front of the Center, you're not going to get close to the man unless you've spent time together at a construction site. Tsukamoto liked working with concrete and looked for jobs in that area; I, on the other hand, was on the lookout for signboards posting odd jobs and cleanup work. We each knew who the other was, but we did not exchange words for the first six or seven years. Someone like me, of course, who was none too popular and was frequently ignored by others on the street, didn't get on familiar terms very easily with most men even on the job. There were more than a few days when I'd make the long wait in front of the Center until 6:00 a.m. alone, without speaking to anyone.

About the time when it became necessary to take any job offered by the Center regardless of the content, I ended up on the same construction site with Tsukamoto and got to know him better. I can't remember the exact incident, but something about his personality made an indelible impression on me.

This was one man who apparently felt no compulsion whatsoever to get the better of someone else and enjoy the momentary ego boost that resulted. Nearly everyone in San'ya I've gotten to know (not just those who come to the Center) embraces the desire, which is like an incurable disease, to boost his own ego. If the chance to inflate one's pride ever presents itself, few men here will overlook it.

For example, if in the course of conversation a San'ya day laborer discovers that his colleague is misinformed about something, he simply cannot suppress the words, "What, you didn't even know that?!" And if that colleague (usually me) is found to be wanting in some department at the work site, he is normally shown up by his fellow day laborer, who generally misses no opportunity to demonstrate how much better he is than his colleague (that is, me). The reason for this, I think, boils down to a lack of self-confidence on the part of most day laborers. That they feel compelled to confirm their superiority, to themselves and their peers, on every occasion that arises must be because comporting themselves in a serene yet completely self-assured manner is something totally alien to them.

And because I'm no exception to the rule that San'ya day laborers are lacking in self-confidence, I, too, am unable to suppress the desire to pit myself against the person who shows me up at the work site and to lord it over him on some other occasion. In my case, I can't resist the opportunity to rub my superior education in the face of my fellow worker. I, too, have none of that serene yet completely self-assured manner. This lack, I think, is at the heart of the San'ya day laborer's childishness. If you talk to any day laborer (myself included), you'll soon discover a childlike impulsiveness concealed in every one of them—they who, no matter how you look at it, are just ordinary middle-aged or older men. They're all dying to feel superior to the next man.

This naked impulse, there for all to see, lurks in the whole lot of these old men who've been deprived of the experience of tasting the approval of their peers. And so when the chance to boost their egos comes up, they jump at it without shame, like twelve-year-olds.

It took me a while to figure out that what made Tsukamoto special was the absence of any urge toward self-aggrandizement. At first, I simply thought of him as being clearly different from the rest, and was attracted to his demeanor in a nonspecific way.

In Tsukamoto I could detect an air of quiet self-confidence that nearly every other San'ya day laborer clearly lacked (or had lost a long time ago). Here was someone who never tried to pit his own will against the will of others. Yet neither was he one to truckle to other men's views. If he met up with an unacceptable opinion, he would absorb it as if he were a wad of cotton and become completely silent. Offering no opinion of his own was Tsukamoto's way of indicating disagreement. After letting the other man have his say, he would attempt to change the subject without imparting his own views or expressing any dissent. If his opponent still didn't get the message and continued to rant, he would revert to his absorption mode and once again take it all in like a wad of cotton. You just couldn't get Tsukamoto to come out with any words confronting or attacking his opponent. At the same time, he would never yield to his opponent's view.

chapter 3

Tsukamoto wasn't a particularly tall man, but he was certainly tall for his age (sixty or thereabouts) at 172–73 cm (5 ft. 8 in.). What really caught one's eye, though, were the barrel chest, which was much thicker than the ordinary man's, and the bull neck, which made him look like one of those rogue priests from Mount Hiei.[1] Taking him on would surely have required an unusual amount of resolve. But in fact no one tried to pick a fight with Tsukamoto, and of course Tsukamoto never picked a fight with anyone else. There was an air of absolute peace and tranquillity about the man. This aura was most pleasant for anyone associated with it, and a group of men always seemed to surround him.

Anyway, I ended up with Tsukamoto at the same work site and we eventually got to talking. Later, Tsukamoto approached me and sought me out as a partner in conversation. He had his reasons: specifically, he was interested in some reliable information about ghosts. I myself didn't believe in ghosts. Tsukamoto was in a situation where he was anxious to deny the existence of ghosts but was not able do so unequivocally. He wanted to probe my own grounds for refuting their existence.

"Well . . ." I began, "I guess there's no way you can actually deny that ghosts exist or have the power to haunt people, but when you look at the situation from the standpoint of the use value that the fear of ghosts has, then I think there is plenty of reason to doubt their existence."

This was not something we talked about while waiting in front of the Center in the early morning. Tsukamoto and I were both careful to avoid provoking suspicion among our peers, and we steered our conversation clear of sensitive topics such as this when we were at the Center. We'd get started up when we met on the street and Tsukamoto began asking me questions, such as, "So, Ōyama-san, why aren't *you* afraid of ghosts?" Tsukamoto didn't like people visiting him in his own room, and knowing this, I never set foot in his doya. Our conversations always took place on the street. Sometimes they lasted a couple of hours.

"People actually have a need to be afraid, for some reason. That's what I think. Our fear of ghosts is grounded in some psychological need. People just couldn't stand living in a terror-free world. Let me put it the other way around: if there were something out there *really* terrifying, then our fear of ghosts would go flying out the window.

"War can be the source of utter terror," I went on, "but not always. So let's think, for example, about living under a totalitarian regime. There'd be no telling when the secret police would be knocking on your door, or when someone in your family would get hauled away, never to return. You'd live, day after day, in sheer terror of this sort of thing happening. So would you be afraid of ghosts at a time like that?"

Tsukamoto said nothing.

"Of course you wouldn't. You're frightened enough as it is, just coping with everyday life, so you're hardly going to be fazed by an evil spirit or two. People's fear of evil spirits just fills a psychological need for a surrogate when no true object of terror exists in their daily lives. That's my feeling. People couldn't cope with a life in which fear was completely absent. That's why they come up with ghost stories."

Tsukamoto, who had remained silent and wore the same expression he did when listening to an opinion he couldn't countenance, eventually, over the space of several conversations on the street, elaborated on his situation.

We who lived in San'ya and worked as day laborers would of course have to die right here in San'ya as well. Tsukamoto wanted to make very sure that word of his death never found

its way to his next of kin. I never asked Tsukamoto whom he
left behind when he came here, and he never told me. Did he
marry, have children, and then leave them? Or did he, like me,
never have a family and simply become estranged from his
parents and siblings? I simply don't know.

One thing for certain is that Tsukamoto was petrified, not
so much by the thought of his body being placed in the cus-
tody of his parents or other family members after he died, but
by the very possibility that news of his death would reach
them at all. He wanted nothing more than to vanish from this
world without his family or relatives ever learning about it. (I
haven't a clue as to why this was so important for him.)

That being the case, Tsukamoto said he'd never take part in
any activity that might get him involved with the police. He
hadn't established residency here (as I had), and as long as he
kept out of trouble, his whereabouts wouldn't be reported to
his relatives while he was alive. The problem was what would
happen after he had died. Tsukamoto said that the police
would almost certainly attempt to ascertain his identity in the
event of death by illness or accident. When applying for his
white card[2] at the Tamahime Employment Agency nearly
twenty years ago, he merely wrote down a local address (now
one must establish formal residency with the city ward), and it
was unlikely that his identity could be determined from that
source alone. But he was worried that, given the thoroughness
of the Japanese police, they would eventually figure out his
family background if he died in San'ya.

Tsukamoto even told me this: Before coming to San'ya, he
had work done on his teeth by a dentist in his home province
(I didn't ask where). What if the dental records from that time
(some thirty years ago) were compared to an impression taken
after his death? (Tsukamoto said that his teeth were strong

and hadn't changed much, although you'd think they'd have worn down a bit after thirty years.) That might be all the police needed, he said.

It was not nearly enough, Tsukamoto said, merely to entertain the hope that his body would be disposed of anonymously without his relatives being informed. What could he do to increase the probability—to the point where he could live at peace with himself—of being buried without his identity ever being discovered? This one thought, he confessed, had preoccupied him for years on end.

The decision that he had arrived at was to take his own life in the primeval forests of Aokigahara.[3] Even the Japanese police, upon finding his bleached skeleton in that forest with no identifying papers, would be unable to ascertain who he was. If, in fact, they *were* able to do so, well, that was that; he'd resign himself, he said. (Resign himself to what, I wondered?) The simple knowledge that he had done his best would sustain his resignation. (But whose resignation, exactly—the *dead* Tsukamoto's?) That's how far his resolve had taken him, he told me. But something had shaken his resolve: namely, the fear of ghosts (or rather, the possibility of ghosts) hovering over Aokigahara's primeval forests.

I was flabbergasted. (Is the man serious? I wondered.)

"So what's wrong with that?" I said. "You're going to become an evil spirit yourself, you know. You'll have plenty of company, too, and at least you won't be lonely. Things could be a lot worse." So I argued, but the cloud on Tsukamoto's face did not dissipate.

I was at a loss to explain to him just how irrational it was to be so apprehensive about one's condition after death. Tsukamoto, for his part, allowed that it was all a bit absurd.

"Yet the fact remains, I can't die in peace because of the worry this is causing me. There's just no getting around it."

40

chapter 3

Actually, Tsukamoto never said this in so many words. He was simply not disposed to argue with people. It was obvious what he was thinking, however, from the expression on his face.

"I don't believe in an afterlife," I told him another time, "but if I did become a ghost, I'd still want to keep to myself even after I died. So I for one wouldn't be running around trying to haunt people. . . . And besides, during the short period you *were* still alive in Aokigahara, you'd have very little time for a face-off with ghosts. So why fret about it even if they do in fact exist and really do haunt people? You wouldn't be human much longer at that point anyway. You'd be one of them soon enough, right?"

It could be that Tsukamoto's fear of ghosts was just an excuse. Wasn't he in fact using his conversation with me as a means of solidifying his resolve to do away with himself at Aokigahara? Or was his fear actually quite deeply ingrained? And was I, who simply couldn't get serious about this sort of thing, making light of something about which he was genuinely afraid?

Tsukamoto was an inveterate gambler. No mere weekend racetrack aficionado, he tried his hand at virtually every form of betting. I am quite certain that he had no savings. Tsukamoto offered few details, but he surely must have poured his entire earnings, aside from the money he spent on food and shelter, into his habit. His lifestyle was no doubt typical of the San'ya gambling addict.

There seems to be little doubt that Tsukamoto's life went to pieces because of his habit; yet gambling was so important to him, and his character so intimately linked with it, that just to look at him you could scarcely believe that it could be such a terrible vice.

For someone who poured most of his earnings into gambling and was most likely sustaining heavy losses every month, Tsukamoto was a man of surprisingly few moods. He suffered his losses with aplomb, day by day, week by week, month by month. He was one of many day laborers who essentially worked to support his habit; yet when someone gave himself over to a vice as completely as he did (to the degree that it formed an integral part of his character), it no longer even seemed like a vice. Tsukamoto's gambling had indeed attained that level, to my way of thinking. Far from corrupting him, it seemed rather to have nourished his spirit. And as a crucial ingredient of that spiritual makeup, his gambling had been transformed, in my mind at least, into something quite admirable.

It was highly unusual for a man of Tsukamoto's generation to register no interest in baseball or sumo wrestling, but he was one of the few who did not. His life was completely taken up with horse racing, bicycle racing, boat racing, and automobile racing, and there was simply no room for any other interest. He recognized the likes of Nagashima, Oh, and Inao (insofar as they were the names of famous baseball players), but he really didn't have the faintest idea who they were.[4]

Tsukamoto was a superstar among the Center regulars. A natural air of nobility pervaded his looks, his character, and his actions. This nobility, moreover, transmitted itself even to the most dull-witted of observers. If you hadn't heard the name Tsukamoto, you'd be regarded as a sham by Center regulars and wouldn't be taken seriously.

For years Tsukamoto invariably worked for cash (that is, a day's pay for a day's labor), but he switched to contract work (that is, long-term labor) about a year ago. It became apparent that by working for cash alone as a regular day laborer he could no longer collect the twenty-six unemployment insurance stamps in a two-month period that were necessary to receive his unemployment dole. When applying for contract work, he put himself down as fifty-two years old. Long-term labor has a stricter age limit than daily labor, and Tsukamoto, who was actually around sixty, would never be hired were he to give his real age. The age limit for this sort of work was fifty-five. In some cases it was fifty, and on occasion it was just forty-five. Center officials knew that Tsukamoto wasn't really fifty-two, but their only charge was to copy down what Tsukamoto had written in on his registration card, and so they never bothered him about it. By-the-day jobs for cash sometimes have an age limit as well, although it is a rarity; so I fudge the age on my registration card by three years, just in case. Some men use an alias.

The young Kodama was one of those who may have been using an alias, although I don't know for sure. Kodama would show up at the Center around the same hour I did. He was a colorful figure. He dyed his long hair brown and wore a purple jacket with a dragon embroidered on the back. He also wore a white headband (not a bandana) tightly wound around his forehead. When it got light enough to see, you could make out the characters embroidered on it: "Yui: My Life." He informed us that he was an officer in Asaka Yui's fan club.[5] Kodama first started showing up at the Center about five or six years ago, but even then Asaka Yui must have already passed the age when she could be called a teen idol.

He was one of those people who couldn't keep quiet even for a moment, and he chatted indiscriminately with whomever was around him. At first I thought him to be in his late twenties, but the Center work sheet he had on him showed his age to be thirty-six. This age was correct, he told me. He would commute to the work site in the same outfit he wore to the Center, minus the headband. Once he donned his work clothes, however, he was transformed into a serious laborer and applied himself diligently to every task. Kodama came to the Center for about three years, but he is no longer around.

Masked Man is another person who stopped coming to the Center after the by-the-day cash jobs dried up. Not only did he never remove his small surgical mask, even for a moment, he actually covered his cheeks with a dirty cotton towel (a Japanese one, made of muslin, not terry cloth).

The only parts of his face exposed to the outside world were his forehead, as far down as the eyes, and his mouth, down to the chin. (Unlike most people who wear a mask when they have a cold, he did not cover his mouth.) Not only was the middle of his face completely covered up by the mask, his profile was totally obscured by the towel covering his cheeks. If you took a good look, you could see the glint radiating from a pair of crafty eyes. (Granted, this impression is the result of having observed him later at the work site.)

I don't think he ever changed either the mask or the muslin towel covering his cheeks. That is, he never showed up wearing a brand-new, pristine white mask or towel. Still, he must have washed them both periodically, because although they were soiled, they didn't give off a foul smell. To the bystander, however, they looked dirty enough as they were. His clothes were no better, either, looking very shabby even by San'ya standards.

Masked Man came to the Center for about four or five years to get work, and I was at the same work site with him

many times. I never did get a glimpse of his entire face, however. There were complaints about this at the Center, I understand, and I heard that officials there instructed him more
than once to remove his mask. He was adamant, however,
and refused to take it or the towel off. He wore them at the
Center; he wore them at work; he wore them going to work.
Masked Man was always "in uniform."

He was never "out of uniform," moreover, no matter how
hot the season. Yet here was a man who, whenever I spoke
with him, I found to be very savvy. He was extremely well informed without being judgmental, deeply conversant with social issues and highly cognizant of his own present standing in
society. (I would not be at all surprised if I were told that he
once held an important position in some firm. He was probably in his late fifties.) He did not live in the *doyagai,* but
commuted to San'ya by train in the early morning.

He certainly was possessed of an enormous ego. He may
not have been the sort who stopped at nothing, however fla-
grant, to show off his superiority, but he was always ready
with a barb for someone else whenever the chance arose.

"So, Ōyama-san, your hobby is saving money? What are
you going to do with it, build a house?"

This is the sort of thing he would say. He liked to talk. And
he kept his mouth uncovered so that he could talk at will. His
mask covered his face from just below the eyes down to the
tip of his nose, but his lips were always exposed to air. This
was not the ordinary position for face masks, but it certainly
conformed to his penchant for talking.

Masked Man was not the sort who tried to get the better of
someone while on the job, at least in any obvious way, but he
was always maneuvering to get the upper hand while appear-

ing to defer to the other person. That is how it was when I found myself together with him at the work site. On those occasions when we had to find out from the manager or whoever was in charge what to do next, I was always the one who had to ask, because he never made himself available for instructions. And yet he wasn't about to take orders from me. It was easy to lose patience with a workmate like him.

I recall thinking to myself constantly, "Masked Man, someone like you can ill afford to complain about discrimination!" (It was not possible, I decided, that the man suffered any physical defect requiring the use of a mask and face towel. On the contrary, I was absolutely certain that his need for the mask and towel was purely psychological.) "You have no reason to denounce people who discriminate against you!" I was just itching to tell him something like this. As far as I was concerned, the price he had to pay for enjoying the freedom of donning a mask and towel was becoming the object of people's ridicule. Discrimination against someone like Masked Man was only natural, I thought.

Masked Man's odd penchant for the stinging rebuke in response to any attempt to treat him like an ordinary human being was unforgivable, to my way of thinking. There were times when all I wanted to do was vent my prejudice against him, because he was in effect courting such discrimination with his own deeds. When he was cutting me down with his digs and his sarcasm, I wanted nothing more than to snap back at him, "Listen, you're the crazy one!" But he disappeared before I ever worked up the nerve. I guess I must have been nursing some pent-up grudge that needed an adversary. Someone possessed of a quiet self-confidence, like Tsukamoto-san of Aokigahara fame, would, I am sure, never even have lifted an eyebrow at anything that Masked Man said.

Ogata-san, a former roof-tile worker, wouldn't have, either.

Ogata was not as genial as Tsukamoto. He would wait quietly in front of the Center until 6:00 a.m., whiling away the hours without saying a word to anyone. He was a stout, robust man in his late forties. Masked Man was one of the very few people with whom he chose to speak at all.

Ogata got into a fistfight on three different occasions in front of the Center. (There may have been other times; these are the fights I witnessed.) He emerged the victor all three times, but after his opponent ran off, he, too, yielded his place in line (I was the benefactor once) and left the premises himself. On just one occasion the man who fled after getting beaten by Ogata reappeared with three or four other men; Ogata obviously knew what to expect. He was accustomed to defending himself.

He was on very good terms with Masked Man. The latter doubtless sensed my aversion toward him, and warmed up to Ogata in order to spite me. A person cannot be gentle if he lacks strength; nor can he embrace others if he is not himself brimming with quiet self-confidence. Like Tsukamoto, Ogata indeed had that capacity for gentleness and for embracing his fellow man. He was the epitome of manliness, insofar as he could take on some onerous task with a stoic reluctance that spoke of great personal sacrifice. He didn't have that air of placid serenity that Tsukamoto had, but he cut the more manly figure.

It is not only fitting but also perfectly natural for a man to approach an unwelcome task at the work site with an attitude of stoic self-sacrifice. If it were me, however, I'd doubtless be itching to flaunt my good deed: "Look, everybody, see how gallant I am!" Such emotion, of course, undermines the very virtue one wishes to uphold, but it wells up in me nonetheless.

All of which is to say that I was never cut out for such gallantry.

In its most basic form at the work site, gallantry begins with deciding who will take orders from the work site manager or other person in charge. If you're on your own, you're it, of course. The problem starts when two or more men are working together. A man named Iwata was a fine example of someone utterly devoid of manliness, because he always managed to stay out of the line of fire. He commuted to the Center most diligently in his quest for unemployment insurance stamps, but he'd never put himself in harm's way while on the job. And to make matters worse, he would spout an endless stream of vulgar and tasteless jokes while waiting in the early morning for the Center to open.

In the eyes of Tsukamoto, who yearned to disappear in Aokigahara, or of Ogata, the former roof-tile worker, I must have looked very much like Iwata did to me. The word *mien* comes to mind as I reflect on all this, and I am reminded of just how difficult it is to label myself a man of noble mien when recalling the likes of Tsukamoto, Ogata, and Kinoshita (the man who volunteered to dig ditches under the blistering sun).

I do not doubt that men of noble mien exist even among the ranks of religious groups and extremist factions, but in my eyes neither Tanaka-san, a member of the Sōka Gakkai, nor Katō-san, a one-time radical activist, both of whom I encountered at the Center, could be numbered among them.

Tanaka zealously tried to convert me before one of the national elections, but he finally realized that he was getting nowhere.[6] After that, he would simply ask me over and over,

"Say, are you feeling all right?" *A sinner like you who refuses to join our congregation is bound to meet up sooner or later with some calamity—perhaps you have already?* His words conveyed this veiled threat. When I replied (smiling to myself, of course), "Actually, I haven't been doing all that well lately," he regarded me with a glint in his eye. That's the sort of person he was: a man so obsessed with his personal salvation that he didn't realize what a miserable figure he cut.

I first got to know Katō, the former activist, when I was living on the streets in Shinjuku. (For a short period right before moving to San'ya, I did construction work out of Takadanobaba and slept in Shinjuku Station.[7]) I decided to come to San'ya after first learning about the place from him. He was a year or two younger than I and still possessed a striking countenance that spoke of his being a ladies' man during his youth. Katō didn't live in San'ya, but he would make an occasional appearance at the Center when he was in the market for contract work. Not willing to give up his former political life completely, he also involved himself in San'ya labor union activities.

Katō was a husband and a father. His wife was a dependable, well-educated woman who worked as a caddy at a golf course. The couple lived in a good-sized city on the Kantō Plain outside Tokyo, in one of those large apartment complexes put up by the Japan Housing Corporation. He usually worked near his home in some construction job, either as a day laborer or as a contract laborer (he was doing scaffolding work when I first met him), but he sometimes visited San'ya in search of a job from the Center recruiting office.

This was a man of extraordinary strength, energy, and intelligence—hardly one to associate with the likes of me—but when I first got to know him he had already sunk into the depths of alcoholism. I couldn't be sure, being able to gaze at him only from afar, but I always wondered if Katō had designs on starting some political movement in San'ya. More than once I observed him engaging in what looked like a feud with union activists.

I'd meet up with Katō whenever he made one of his forays from out of town to the Center recruiting office, where I was usually camping out early in the morning. Already inebriated even at 3:00 or 4:00 a.m., he would face the sky and bellow some political slogan. If he saw someone he knew he would sponge some change for another drink. Paying no heed to the scowls of his peers, he would put on a desperate face until he managed to extract a few coins. I, too, was one of those from whom he would solicit the price of a drink.

What was the true source of his despondency? I believe that he was deeply hurt by the fact that the radical leftists he associated with never took him seriously or offered him the kind of position in their infrastructure he felt he deserved. He found himself unable to play the role of foot soldier with men young enough to be his children in order to reactivate his political career in San'ya; yet at the same time he couldn't face old age as a common day laborer. Both prospects were equally unbearable to him. Was this not how his despondency manifested itself: in the form of these early-morning bellows in front of the Center?

Exposing his drunken figure on the streets of San'ya for all to see, Katō obviously wanted to appear in the eyes of anyone who knew him or ran into him a most destitute and downtrodden character. Downtrodden though he might have been, however, he was far from destitute. His wife, who had also once been active in the leftist movement, had all kinds of connections, and if he ever fell into truly straitened circumstances, he would doubtless get help from that quarter. Meanwhile,

Katō had not broken all his ties with his siblings and relatives, who wielded considerable power in their rural base. He may not have achieved the position he considered his due in the world—I'm inclined to say "business"—of radical activism, but in the eyes of us who are truly destitute here in San'ya, he might as well have been a member of the elite. He could never have seriously entertained the fear that he would live out his twilight years as a homeless person on the streets foraging for a meal. Watching him get blind drunk and rage at the heavens, I couldn't help mumbling to myself, "Aren't you the lucky one!"

Although his intellect dwarfed those of Tsukamoto and Ogata, Katō possessed no gallantry, exhibited no gentility or strength of character, and had a completely undeveloped sense of resignation in spite of his fifty years. He was, in short, a spoiled, middle-aged alcoholic, and nothing more. He didn't even realize that the thing he was dying to possess amounted merely to an elevated position in what was in fact a kind of business. He seemed to believe, moreover, that any base or scandalous ideology associated with this "business" could be cleansed by the beautiful leftist ideals he still embraced. What a lout, I mumbled to myself, practically spitting out the words.

Saitō-san, who belonged to an older generation of leftists than Katō (he is now about sixty-five years old), became a dropout from society after he got involved in a labor dispute during his tenure as junior executive at a provincial bank. Unlike Katō, he was a sincere, hard-working laborer. Although he possessed none of the former's spoiled, downtrodden nature, he was in his own way a most singular human being, albeit entirely different from Katō. In addition to working as a tobi, he also worked (I was to learn later) at a hanba as a contracting firm's principal accountant.

When first I met up with Saitō on a job I got through the Center recruiting office, he was in his late fifties and looked like a typical scaffolding worker, yet he struck me immediately as being quite unlike your run-of-the-mill tobi. We who served as his assistants would hand him whatever he needed for his scaffolding work, just as with any other tobi. Right away, however, I detected a difference in him: his manner of speaking.

He used very polite speech to me and the other assistants. It wasn't all that noticeable while on the job. He might say something like, "Would you please bring me the ——? Take your time." (Even this manner of speaking, however, was enough to set him apart from the other tobi.) During the rest periods and lunch breaks, however, his conversations with us were laced with honorific language. We all thought it extremely peculiar, but it was hardly a matter to complain about, so we accepted it in silence.

I lost touch with him for a while after that, but when he joined us as a Center recruit two or three years later, this time as a common laborer (he would have been too old to continue as a tobi), we worked together as equals on several occasions.

At the time, Saitō was living in an apartment, which consisted of a single three-mat room near the Jōban Line.[8] Once we worked at a construction site close to the apartment, and at his invitation, I stopped by his room on the way home for a desultory chat. During this, the first casual conversation I'd ever had with him, I encountered his fierce anti-authoritarianism and was a bit taken aback, but I offered no rebuttal. Saitō, after all, was a former tobi, whose skills were of an entirely higher order than my own. Whenever working with him at a construction site, I always felt obliged to defer to him. I knew enough about the ways of the world not to cross him now.

chapter 3

I learned that when he was still working for the provincial
bank, Saitō took a wife and fathered a child, then abandoned them both. In the course of several conversations, the
honorific forms he once used to address me disappeared,
and his language reverted to a style more appropriate to the
fourteen- or fifteen-year difference in our ages. For my part,
I began vigorously rebutting his anti-authoritarian stance;
and when that happened, our relationship fell apart. He was
an anti-Establishmentarian of the old school who believed
that one's character and one's political inclination were in-
divisible. To Saitō, I apparently came across as someone
with deep character flaws because I harbored no rage
against the iniquities of the general contractors and the bureaucrats.

Maybe Saitō was in fact broad-minded enough to accept
men of character who were not against the Establishment; if
so, then I must have come off as someone who not only
sucked up to the Establishment but who possessed a base
character as well. Either way, he curled his lips in contempt at
my rebuttals.

"We look at the world in fundamentally different ways,
Saitō-san. I judge the anti-Establishmentarians, including you,
according to a standard of intelligence and have concluded
that you're a fool. Meanwhile, you judge Establishmentarians
like me according to a standard of morality and have found
me to be wicked."

Saitō was outraged at my words. His hair positively stood
on end.

"Get out!" he yelled. "I will not breathe the same air as
you!" And I was tossed out of his three-mat apartment onto
the street at 2:00 a.m.

Our rifts would not last more than a month or two, however. Sooner or later we'd begin exchanging greetings at the

Center. And then the pattern would repeat itself: the conversations we had would eventually lead to discussions about
politics and society, and before you knew it we'd have another falling out. I think we were both starving for the opportunity to lecture people about politics. Neither of us could
suppress the desire to speak out: Saitō with his anti-
Establishment views; I with my *anti*-anti-Establishment ones.
Mouthing words having to do with politics and society, even
though we knew it would end in a rift, was something we
both simply could not resist.

Conversation can be enjoyable. The political discussions
Saitō and I had with each other did indeed have their pleasurable moments, even though we knew they would result in an
impasse. This is probably why we never broke off completely.
Saitō's eccentricity was not limited, however, to his unusual
obsession with politics. It manifested itself in other ways as
well.

Two or three years ago, for example, when he had passed
the age of sixty and found it increasingly difficult to get work,
Saitō decided to starve himself to death. After spending three
weeks on the slopes of Mount Takao[9] and sustaining himself
only with water, however, he realized that was not going to
succeed and finally returned to San'ya. This is what he told
me (and not just me, I'm quite sure). He was so emaciated
when I saw him that he looked like a different person (and
this was after he'd already spent time in the hospital on government welfare and regained his strength). When I asked
him, "What on earth happened?" he related this story about
his campaign to starve himself on Mount Takao. He must
have been telling the truth.

Here is another example. After setting aside a minimal
amount of his earnings for his own livelihood, he gave away

the rest to other people. He would tell them that he was
"lending" it to them (for the sake of appearances, I suppose),
but in fact he wanted to give it away. He would even steer
the conversation in the direction of his listener's finances in
an effort to come up with some excuse to give ("lend")
money to the person. He tried this tack on me, too, and at
first I was upset because I didn't know what he was getting
at.

I secretly referred to Saitō as a "One-Man Salvation Army."
He would tell the person he'd lent money to, "Return it when
you can. I'm in no hurry." But when someone actually *did* attempt to return the money, Saitō would refuse to take it
back—or so I heard from a man who had tried.

After being hospitalized upon his return from the moun-
tains, Saitō was lucky enough to become a permanent welfare
recipient, and so he remains. His penchant for "lending"
money persists unabated, despite the fact that his money
comes from the government.

Whenever I asked him, "Is the One-Man Salvation Army
still in business?" he would take great offense and reply, "No,
no, you've it all wrong! An old man like me can't use the
money, and there are people right before my eyes who need it
in the worst way. I'm happy they can use it. That's what
money's for."

Saitō's response sounded rather defensive, and I don't believe that it reflected how he truly felt. I could tell that he was
enjoying himself thoroughly. It was his way of demonstrating
his authority, I concluded. Was he not satisfying his lust for
power through the emotional highs he incited in others,
watching them become buoyant after he gave them money? If
it were true that he really didn't need the money and sincerely
wanted to hand it over to those who did, then he could have

simply put some money in the pockets of men sleeping on the street without attracting anyone's notice. Granted, Saitō's lust for power was indeed the most benevolent sort, but a lust for power it certainly was, just the same. That's why I called him a "One-Man Salvation Army."

My conversations with Saitō inevitably led to a falling out because he lacked the easygoing nature required to forgive my slovenly ways, while I lacked the tolerance needed to overlook the stubbornness and shallowness of his anti-Establishment views. Each time Saitō denounced the general contractors, or the Finance Ministry, or the ex-bureaucrats who assumed high positions in private corporations, I would rally to their defense with every argument at my disposal. And when I did so, his rage against the general contractors and the Finance Ministry and the ex-bureaucrats would find a new target in the character of the person who defended them. For my part, I would never back down from attacks of this sort, no matter what aspersions he cast on my despicable character or however much he curled his lips in contempt.

"There's really nothing more frightening than allowing a self-righteous person like you to hold power," I told him. "I have yet to meet up with any misfortune on account of a general contractor or the Finance Ministry or a high-ranking bureaucrat, but I shiver to think of what would happen if someone like you, who never even doubts his own morals, seized power. Don't you know your history? The world is much better off when it is plagued with minor evils."

"You mean to say that things like collusion among the big construction firms and graft in the Finance Ministry are minor evils?"

"That's right, they're minor," I told him, launching into my counterattack. "It's self-righteous people like you who bring about real catastrophe. The inveterate do-gooders are the ones who bring the world to grief." (I was, of course, secretly making sport of Mr. "One-Man Salvation Army.") "Don't you know how much evil has been committed by the likes of Mao Zedong and Pol Pot?"

At that point I got my final dig in: "I hope you enlighten yourself to this fact before you die, at least." I am truly devoid of all virtue. No wonder the other men don't even bother to greet me on the street.

Saitō, the "One-Man Salvation Army," has retired from construction work and now leads the good life on welfare. In the days when he was still among us, jostling for position in front of the Center gate, he was sometimes hailed by Endō-san, who would show up in front of the Center and ask him, "Want to come along?" Saitō almost invariably broke ranks and followed him. Sometimes I'd be asked too, when more than one man was called for. This was when jobs were already becoming scarce, and I would tag along gladly. Endō was a construction worker, not a street agent, but once in a while he was ordered to recruit men himself. Men in this position are not that uncommon in San'ya.

Murota-san was another one who did this sort of thing, and he frequently swung by the Center, among other places, to find recruits. This was in the days before the recession, however, and he apparently had a hard time of it. I never once gave him a second glance myself. He did not have a trade and was what you call a "ditchdigger" or "miscellaneous worker," which is to say a common laborer, and nothing more; yet he was as skilled as any specialist in every aspect of construction work (or so it appeared to me). Common laborer though he may have been, he was a real pro.

Murota is about sixty now, so he must have been in his midfifties when he began working full-time as a day laborer five or six years ago. He had the air of a hot-blooded youth in his prime. A small and slender man, he was also wiry and muscular, and thus seemingly possessed of great physical strength. He had mastered all phases of construction work, it is true; but the first thing you noticed about him was his short fuse. I often wondered how someone of his temperament ever made it as a recruiter or a site manager, and when I told him so, he said, "I don't pick fights with people under me." I never asked him if coming to blows with his superiors didn't have the same end result of hindering his work, but he did show me a scar once on his side where he'd been stabbed with the sharp end of a ratchet used in scaffolding after getting into a fight with a tobi. He was the victim in this case, of course, but I can't imagine him not being the perpetrator on at least a few occasions.

One time Murota was reprimanded for being late to work, by a site manager who looked as if he were barely out of high school. An irate Murota was ready to pounce on the fellow when I managed to pinion his arms from behind. This was nearly four years ago. It was my fault in a way, because I had gotten there on the early side, and the discrepancy between our arrival times was all too obvious. The construction site was a small one, located right at the top of the stairs leading out of Roppongi Station.[10] I guess there were too few laborers present to conduct the usual roll call and pep talk before work, and so none took place. If it had, then the tardy Murota might have had enough time to change into his work garb without anyone noticing.

I had already started work, having received my orders from the youthful site manager, when I heard Murota embroiled in

58

an altercation with the manager near the work site entrance.
I went over to take a look and saw Murota, still in his street
clothes, flinging his bag to the ground and making ready to
lunge at his superior. After sneaking up on Murota and pin-
ioning him from behind, I did my best to calm him down,
whispering, "OK, Murota, that's it for today. Go on home."
Surprisingly, he agreed without a fuss. A volatile temper he
may have had, but apparently it didn't take much to douse the
fire. This was the last time I worked with Murota. I don't believe that this incident was the reason for it, but he never
showed up at the Center after that.

I ran into Murota riding a bicycle on a San'ya street just a
couple of years ago. We exchanged greetings, and he told me
that he was getting his work from some place other than the
Center recruiting office. I saw him another time, again on his
bicycle, just six months ago. "I've given up on working," he
told me. "I don't go to construction sites any more. I only do
those jobs hired out by the Tokyo metropolitan government.
I can get by without doing any real work now." His countenance had grown quite mellow, and his body seemed to have
shrunk. Then it hit me: Getting through times like these with
Murota's temperament must be very difficult indeed.

At that point Murota was living in a tiny hut he had built
somewhere along the Arakawa Canal, well to the east of
San'ya. "So, you're still making a go of it, eh?" Murota said
to me, by way of encouragement. I didn't know how to answer him.

Ikeno-san showed up at the Center about four or five years
after I started getting my work there. It was his first taste of
the laboring life, and he worked as a common day laborer out

of the Center for about a year. Ikeno, who was two or three years younger than I, told me he used to work for a brokerage firm and showed me his old company ID. He encouraged me to invest every bit of savings I had in equities. This was before the stock market crashed.

Ikeno was a very agreeable sort who always deferred to me, his senior in this line of work, simply because I happened to have seven or eight years' experience on him, counting my years in Kamagasaki. I was on the job with him twice at different construction sites, and I must say that although he was possessed of a disposition quite unlike that of Tsuka-moto, Ikeno nevertheless had about him that same air of quiet self-confidence. Such men stand out in San'ya. His singular personality is firmly engraved in my memory.

After only about a year he stopped coming to the Center. Three years later, when I met up with him at a construction site, our roles were reversed: Ikeno, now a tobi, was ordering us Center recruits around as his assistants. He was a sensitive, mild-mannered man, however, who never raised his voice. "Well, how are you? It's been a long time." This was how he greeted me; yet it was still an awkward moment. Although well into his middle years, he had retained his athlete's build. He was good at everything. There are tobi who work by the day and others who work on contract at a hanba, but Ikeno was attached to a single firm.

Sometime after that, I saw Ikeno in the driver's seat of a Toyota Land Cruiser, waiting for the signal at Namidabashi intersection. He was with a fairly good-looking, slim-figured woman of about forty. Our eyes met, and I was compelled to give him a silent bow. Ikeno responded magnanimously with a nod, and waved his hand.

Ikeno was also someone who, for a very brief period, tried

his hand at recruiting for his firm men coming to the Center. This is when there was still some work to be had. When he saw me in line, he came up and greeted me. "Sorry for trying to push you into the stock market," he said. Talented yet modest, very capable on his own yet a model of cooperation: this is the sort of man who becomes a leader, I had to confess. (Needless to say, I myself did not think to accept the invitation to work for him.)

Tobi are the aristocrats of San'ya. In the same way that it is possible, in Europe, to distinguish the aristocracy from the common folk by how they look, so it is possible to distinguish tobi from common day laborers by their appearance (their faces more than their physique). The training required to nurture their skills to a level worthy of their calling and the confidence gained through having those skills recognized by their peers give them a commanding presence and bestow on their countenances a certain poise. All in all they cut a very dashing figure. There is a certain crispness about their movements and indeed about their entire demeanor. I would imagine that their individual abilities vary considerably, but the best have a truly unmistakable aura about them. One can tell at a glance: yes, this man, without question, is a tobi.

Carpenters and ironworkers are not employed as day laborers or as contract laborers, so there are none in San'ya. Here, the word *shokunin*—skilled worker—means only one thing, and that is tobi. Men like Saitō (Mr. "One-Man Salvation Army") and Ikeno (the former stockbroker) are exceptions; you could never surmise from their characters what the typical tobi is like. I have never actually met a tobi who treats laborers like slaves, barking at them and driving them into the ground; I have, however, run across several who were proud to the point of arrogance—so much so that they never paid us laborers any heed. (It was as if we never even entered their field of vision.) And I must say that I was not necessarily put off by their arrogant pride.

My hatred of working as a tobi's assistant and being hounded on the job lives side by side with my admiration for the tobi "race." Yet when all is said and done, it seems to me far preferable that the haughty arrogance of these men live on than that it wither away—these men who work closer to death's door than any other group of skilled workers in Japan. There are among tobi some men (although admittedly few in number) who actually consider themselves works of art. I would much rather that such men never vanish from the scene. More and more of late I hear stories of this or that tobi doing the work of a common laborer. I fervently hope that these men—San'ya's very own aristocrats—will be able to ride out this terrible recession. Speaking as a common laborer from San'ya's "plebeian class," I pray that San'ya's spiritual patricians, defending their manly pride and honing their reputations in the face of great danger, manage to survive these hard times and live another day.

This summer (1999) was marked by two incidents. In July, Ogata, the former roof-tile worker, got into an argument with one of the site leaders at a hanba he'd been dispatched to from the Center. He ended up hospitalized after being stabbed with a box cutter in his shoulder and on the back of his right hand. The wound in his hand was deep, severing the tendons and nerves and making it impossible for him to bend his fingers. He now lives in a special lodging facility run by the Tokyo metropolitan government and commutes to a rehab clinic. The site leader was arrested, of course, and now faces trial.

chapter 3

The other incident: Tsukamoto, of Aokigahara fame, has disappeared without a trace.

When I met Tsukamoto in front of the Center one day in August right before Obon, I was surprised to learn that he was now making his home in a park in Ōmori.[11] His hernia had been acting up and he was in no condition to work, he said. I knew well enough that he'd never accept aid from others and so didn't offer any, but I urged him to check himself into a free clinic. Dealing with the bureaucracy, however, could result in having to renew contact with his family—something that Tsukamoto had wanted to avoid. "You're not thinking of going to Aokigahara now, are you?" I was afraid to put the question to him, yet it certainly crossed my mind. A month later, one of the Center regulars told me that Tsukamoto said he was about to turn in his white card to the Tamahime Employment Agency and return to his home in the country.

What could this possibly mean? Had he had a change of heart? Could it really be true that Tsukamoto, who was so afraid of reestablishing contact with his family, had now decided to return to his home in the country and had handed in his white card? I actually hoped that he had. I wanted to believe that his iron will had in fact cracked and that he had allowed contact with his family on account of his illness, yet I couldn't suppress the doubt that such a thing was impossible for so stubbornly principled man as he. Tsukamoto: May the rumors about your will's having weakened be true! This is what I am praying these days.

It is autumn now, and two months have gone by since Tsukamoto disappeared.

chapter 4

I Realize the Importance of
Looking after Myself
and Begin Taking Walks

ABOUT the time when jobs were getting more difficult to come by, I got fed up with my early morning trek to the Center and gave up working altogether. I spent one idle day after the next, living off the meager savings I'd socked away during the bubble years. I did absolutely nothing.

I would wake up in the morning and first dispatch breakfast, consuming the rolls or the instant ramen noodles I had bought the day before; then I'd lie on my futon until noon, watching TV or reading a book. My doya has no refrigerator and so it is impossible to stock up on groceries, but I'd store as many items of food as possible at the head of my bed in order to minimize the need to go out.

Unless I got a job in one of the Tokyo metropolitan government's special work projects, I never went out except to shop at the convenience store or local supermarket. Back in the bunkhouse, I would spend the entire day reading a book I'd checked out from the public library or watching the tube. Because I no longer went to the Center, I lost contact with the regulars. I spoke to no one for days on end. Even on days when I worked for the Tokyo metropolitan government, pulling weeds on reclaimed land or cleaning the guardrails on city streets, the circumstances didn't require having a conversation with anyone (the work was child's play compared to construction work), and so I had none.

No verbal exchange took place even when I paid for my bunk at the front desk. I'd just mumble, "Five" (five nights), or "Seven" (seven nights). Those were the only words necessary. "OK," the clerk would answer and hand me the change, if there was any. No real conversation there, either.

In this way I went for weeks on end without using my voice or exercising my vocal cords. When I found myself needing to speak after a long period of silence, I realized that I couldn't talk right. My voice became gravelly and my throat tightened up. Once I ran into a Center regular on my way back from the store or the library and tried to say something. My voice sounded strange. The other person noticed as well. "Do you have a cold?" he asked. "Yes," I said, but of course it wasn't a cold.

After continuing this life for nearly a year I began to sense a change in my physical condition. I didn't let it worry me at first, figuring that it had to do with the chronic disorder in my autonomic nervous system. But I finally decided that something else was going on and paid a visit to the Center clinic, which is located in the same building as the recruiting office, for a free examination, and learned that my blood pressure was elevated. (The high was between 150 and 160 and the low more than 100.) Next I went to a private doctor, who checked my blood sugar level and found that to be high, too. I was handed a pamphlet with a yellow cover, published by the Japan Diabetes Association, and told to limit my calorie intake to 1,800 calories per day. I still didn't change my ways for a while even after that. But a life of complete idle-

ness cannot continue indefinitely, and because the time was
approaching when I had to start up my commute to the Center recruiting office once again, I decided that I needed some
exercise by way of preparation and began taking walks. This
was about five years ago.

Having been inactive for close to a year, at first I got shoe
sore after just thirty minutes of walking. So checking my
watch, I would turn back no matter where I was after fifteen
minutes and head home the way I came. That made for a
thirty-minute round trip. Over time I gradually extended my
range, stretching thirty minutes into forty, and forty minutes
into an hour.

After about two or three months I was walking two hours
at a stretch. By this time my route was pretty well established.
On the days I didn't work, I'd leave the doya when it was just
starting to get dark and head for the Sumida River. I'd follow
it down to Sakura Bridge, cross the river, and go upstream as
far as Shirahige Bridge. Then I'd make a U-turn and walk
back downstream all the way to Kototoi Bridge, where I'd re-
cross the river and either head back to my doya by way of
Matsuya Department Store down in Asakusa or continue up-
river from the bridge and return the same way I came. Either
route made for about a two-hour walk. I was trying to get in
10,000 strides a day, and at my pace of 1,000 strides every
ten minutes, that added up to 12,000 strides in two hours; so
I was walking far enough.

Even when I started going to the Center again and was getting work two or three times a week, I'd still get in my daily
walk upon my return, although I went just half the distance.
At this point, I'd be rising at 3:00 a.m. (and sometimes 2:00
a.m.) to go to the Center and returning to my doya, dizzy
with fatigue, at around 6:00 p.m.; but I still didn't give up my

walks. My daily constitutional had obviously become an obsession. It was taking over my life.

I had begun taking greater interest in my diet as well, especially my calorie intake. Whenever I learned about some nutritious food (from the television or a magazine), I would invariably give it a try. For a time I lived a life dedicated to good health. I can't speak for the ordinary citizen, but I imagine that a man who goes to a place like San'ya in search of the healthy life is, well, something of a rarity. The custom of taking walks is highly unusual among San'ya day laborers. But I am quite aware of my eccentricity. One further piece of evidence of that isn't going to set me back.

People often speak of man's three vices: drinking, gambling, and whoring. In San'ya, there is hardly anyone who doesn't drink. I'd say that fewer than a tenth of the day laborers in San'ya are nondrinkers. I myself can't drink a drop. If I happened to get a job pouring concrete and work ended early, the man in charge would often buy cups of sake and cans of beer and pass them around to everyone on the job. I never saw anyone but me pass up a drink.

I'm not much of a gambler either, and that includes *pachinko*.[1] Even during the bubble years, the most I'd ever spend on gambling was the occasional purchase of one of those ridiculously expensive, double-your-money racing tickets—it felt like buying into the lottery—at a few thousand yen a pop. San'ya day laborers who don't gamble or play pachinko also number fewer than 10 percent of the total, I'd say. (Now that work is so much harder to come by, though, I'm sure that the situation has changed drastically.)

As for the last vice—paying for sex—very few in San'ya are

into that. The aging of the day laborer population is generally
thought to be a reason, but I believe that it actually has to do
with the fact that whoring is in fundamental opposition to (or
should I say in competition with) gambling. Habitual gamblers cannot possibly be out buying women unless they have
won big. And when you consider just how rare it is to have
that kind of luck, it's logical to conclude that the majority of
those San'ya day laborers who ruined their lives in the first
place because of gambling have very little interest in sex. Thus
it turns out that I'm in the minority on that front as well. I
count myself among the perhaps 20 percent of San'ya day laborers who do in fact buy women. Drinking, no; gambling,
no; whoring, yes. This has made me a first-rate eccentric
among day laborers. (Given my current income, however, this
situation too will no doubt have to change.)

The addition of "fitness nut" to my résumé, then, should
come as no surprise. I was very much an eccentric long before
embarking on this health kick.

On the days I worked, I'd walk half the usual distance, or
about an hour, on unsteady feet, and then eat dinner. On the
days I didn't work, I'd take the usual two-hour walking
course and then eat. The obsession with my health began to
fade, however, when I learned that this routine was actually
the worst thing possible for controlling my blood sugar level,
because it increased the rate of calorie consumption. I haven't
given up walking altogether since then, but I did stop putting
myself through a forced march after work when I was in a
state of exhaustion and barely able to stand.

Thus, my physical condition returned to "normal"—which
is to say, back to the state where I suffered only an occasional
relapse of my autonomic nervous disorder (once every three
or four months). In short, all that walking did not put an end

to the disorder. Having never expected that it would do so in the first place, however, I was in no way disappointed. And in the meantime, I began to realize that walking was a pleasure in itself.

The promenade along the Sumida River is used for walking, jogging, and cycling. During my walks I encountered individuals and groups (sometimes couples) who looked every bit like athletes in an Olympic-style competition. Most of these walkers were extremely serious about their exercise. They were obviously not out there for the sake of a leisurely stroll in order to while away the time. Wearing the uniforms appropriate to their calling and the serious expressions to match, they applied themselves diligently to their task with characteristic form and pace.

The one trait common to nearly all these walkers' form was the pumping motion they made with their arms. They took very long strides, but it was not enough for them to let the momentum of their strides carry over naturally into the swing of their arms. Instead they used an exaggerated motion and consciously led their feet with their arms. They would walk either with fists gripped lightly and elbows bent, or waving their straight arms back and forth like pendulums in the way that kindergarten pupils do when marching in line. This exaggerated motion was a form common to all these "Olympic walkers," it seemed.

It must be noted, however, that this manner of walking is completely unnatural. People don't ordinarily walk with their arms swinging theatrically. So, in order not to be shamed by their own form, they are forced to adopt an attitude of utmost seriousness toward their sport. Only the determined competitor, after all, would even think of undertaking this style of walking!

It is a style that I personally could not accept for the longest time. I simply couldn't get myself out of the habit of walking

69

with long strides and at a fairly good clip, but with one hand
stuffed in my pants pocket. I was embarrassed to reveal any
firmness of purpose in my walking form. I suppose that hiding
my determination in my heart and not revealing it to the
world meant that that I hadn't yet advanced to the stage of
true commitment. Revealing one's determination through
one's form no doubt had its purpose. That exaggerated arm
motion was, I suppose, the final barrier on the path to enlight-
enment about the pleasures of walking for its own sake.

What would happen if one *did* undertake that extremely
unnatural style of walking with arms pumping furiously?
Wouldn't the increased speed and length of stride induced by
such a style further stimulate one's heart and lungs? I don't
know how it works exactly, but the result is that one feels a
faint, pleasant sensation radiating from the upper arms to the
armpits as well as from both sides of the torso and the back.
It is a feeling that made me think, "Well, well, something really good is happening to my body!"

It was nearly three years before I realized that the walking
style employed by a group of middle-aged women (from four to
seven in number) whom I almost invariably encountered during
my outings—a style that resembled kindergartners marching in
line and which made me burst out laughing—was in fact the
correct one and mine was not. This being Japan, these women
and I never exchanged greetings or even nods, despite the fact
that we'd cross paths three to six times a week (I myself was a
middle-aged man, after all, and a day laborer to boot); we simply lowered our gaze and passed each other in silence.

When I first began taking walks along the Sumida River
about five years ago, shacks covered with blue tarpaulins were

already starting to dot the terrace along the riverbank, although their number and density did not compare to what they are now. Today these shacks stand scarcely two or three meters apart and fill the terrace from end to end. From a distance, they look not unlike stalls at a county fair, except that there are far fewer passersby.

Taking a walk or strolling with one's date past that row of shacks requires a good deal of courage. I eventually shifted my own walking course, which went along the riverbank terrace at first, to the promenade on the other side of the concrete dike. I can see why people are reluctant to saunter past those blue-tarp shacks with their occupants camped out in front in small groups.

Once, about four years ago I think (this was when I was still walking along the terrace), I noticed a man who used to stay in the same doya room as I did. Our eyes met and I said hello, but he quickly turned away from me. I had not been particularly friendly with him, but I had sometimes borrowed his bicycle in the morning so that I could turn in my white card to the Tamahime Employment Agency, thus making it possible to receive my unemployment dole later in the day. (The agency window closes at 7:30 a.m., and I would borrow the bicycle if I'd slept in too late to get there in time on foot.) I'd return the favor by buying him a cup of sake or can of beer. That being the case, I naturally felt obliged to greet him, but he obviously felt differently.

I have already touched on the subject of the "special jobs" hired out by the Tokyo metropolitan government; a day laborer with a white card issued by the Tamahime Employment Agency (I was one of them) could apply for these jobs when his number came up.[2] It was possible to get this sort of work once or twice (and sometimes as many as three or four times) a month during the months when it was available, and men with roughly the same registration numbers would end up riding the bus together to the work site.

Thus I got to know Tokunaga-san, a homeless man about my age, through this line of work. The shack he lived in, made of scrap wood and plywood and covered with a blue tarp, was located right below the expressway that runs along the Sumida River's east bank. I'd often pay a visit to Tokunaga's shack on the return leg of my evening walk. The area where he lived was about a ten-minute walk from the row of shacks along the Sumida River terrace.

I'd say that Tokunaga exhibited about the same degree of interest in working as I did. That is, he was always in the market for a job as a day laborer, but he had no intention of working as a contract laborer at a hanba. Thanks to the current recession, he could no longer afford to stay in a doya and took to living in a shack beneath the expressway. As for me, I was just barely able to make it in a doya by living frugally off my meager savings from the bubble era and my occasional income as a day laborer.

With the earnings he received on the days he got work, Tokunaga would buy up large quantities of food: two or three ten-kilogram sacks of rice, canned goods, and prepared food in vacuum-sealed packs (the kind you can heat up in water on a gas burner). I can't eat much rice because of my diabetic condition; in fact, I shouldn't be eating it at all. Tokunaga, in contrast, was a short, slender man with a muscular build and a big appetite, and he always had rice on hand.

His was one of seventy or eighty blue-tarp shacks in the area, which was a veritable shantytown. I knew two other men here besides Tokunaga. Both showed up at the Center on occasion, and I worked with them a number of times at the same construction site. One of the two was a very effeminate homosexual, about fifty years old. I didn't feel comfortable striking up a conversation with him.

The other man, Hasegawa-san, was an extremely diligent day laborer of about forty or so. Even now, during the depths of the Heisei recession, he was under the employ of a single firm and would set out at the same time every day on his bicycle for the commute to his assigned work site. We'd sometimes exchange notes about the job market. Hasegawa's income must have equaled that of any worker his age employed at a small manufacturing firm, but he had been living the life of a homeless person beneath the expressway since the bubble years.

It would have been easy enough for Hasegawa to rent an apartment, since he had no family to support, but he didn't want to be bothered with the expense. This is not to suggest, however, that he was a skinflint. Rather, saving on lodging costs was for him a way to channel that much more money into gambling.

It should be clear from Hasegawa's example that no significant class distinctions obtain between San'ya day laborers living in doya and those living on the street. My income is in fact considerably less than that earned by the "homeless" Hasegawa. As for Tokunaga, who bailed out of his doya and now lives in a tent village, our expenditures are probably quite comparable, if you leave out the money I spend on a bunk. Tokunaga may be "homeless," but this simply means that his base of operations happens to be a blue-tarp shack beneath the expressway. When he is winning big at *pachinko* (specifically, the newer *pachinko*-style slot machines) and gets work for several days running, he'll abandon his shack and spend several weeks, and sometimes upward of two or three months at a stretch, in a doya. There are more than a few "homeless" men who maintain a lifestyle similar to Tokunaga's.

The crucial class distinction in San'ya, then, has nothing to do with having a place to live. Rather, it is based on whether or not you scavenge your food.

Having no permanent abode versus having to forage for a meal—the difference in the degree of misery between the two is great indeed. Tokunaga (like myself) is not willing to take just any job, and he feels little resistance to living on the streets if it comes to that, but if circumstances made him stoop to the level of scrounging garbage, he would resist mightily, I believe. Are not the people in San'ya who are truly homeless those you would call scavengers?

That San'ya's true homeless are the older men who have been wholly excluded from the labor market is apparent from the resistance that they, as former laborers, put up when confronting this ultimate degradation. Those who *can* somehow remain in the labor pool will spare no effort to do so when facing such a crisis. It is only these older men, therefore—men whose final resistance has met with defeat—who are to be counted among the truly homeless.

Welfare benefits are apparently extended to men who have reached a more advanced age (about sixty-five); so the real problem is what might be called the "off-season"—that barren period from the time day laborers leave the labor market until the time they can reap the benefit of welfare. It is the men struggling to make it through this "off-season" who comprise the class of the truly homeless in San'ya, in my view.

The population of scavengers who have crossed San'ya's true class divide will be found in soup lines sponsored by Christian groups and other organizations serving up dumpling stew or rice-and-miso porridge. To the distant observer, they give the impression of men equally dark of skin and mood. Regardless of the season, their clothes are blackened with dirt and their faces deeply tanned from living outdoors. Each man is doubtless possessed of a distinctive personality, but at first glance they all appear to be bound by the same gloomy aspect, the same stony silence. No joke or witty remark emerges from their lips. To a man, they look dark, desolate, and utterly defeated.

A closer look reveals among the ranks a few younger men still in their thirties as well as some robust-looking men in the prime of life, but they somehow go unnoticed by anyone observing casually from a distance.

Clearly, some terrible calamity has visited these men, and they have been unable to withstand the assault—this is the impression one is left with. One can almost hear the grating sound of a heavy weight bearing down on their countenances and their persons. And they look as though they have been crushed by that weight.

Holding numerous bags in both hands or placing them on the ground at their feet, the men wait silently in line for twenty or thirty minutes or longer before finally ingesting a morsel of warm food. (I, too, have waited in line for my share.) The fact that they always carry their bags with them means they do not occupy one of the blue-tarp shacks either on the terrace or beneath the expressway along the Sumida River.

To have any belongings at all, however, is indicative of a will to face the challenge of living outdoors. I don't know what these men do for bedding, but I would imagine that some of them have blankets stored in coin lockers. Having enough blankets at your disposal is by far the most important part of living on the street, albeit the most difficult; a single blanket (which is about all you can walk around with) simply will not ensure a warm, healthful night of sleep outdoors.

Only by laying out a thick mattress of cardboard (at least four or five layers) and sandwiching an extra blanket into one's sleeping bag can one survive a cold winter night in Tokyo. Because it's impossible to move about while carrying all one's clothes and bedding, it is imperative for men living outdoors to find a place to hide their gear. This is not a problem for Tokunaga and the others who have erected their blue-tarp shacks, but those not living in the shanties must continually face the problem of finding a place to stow their bedding.

Wherever you might walk in Tokyo, you can't help noticing the absence of places to hide bedding or other large baggage—and this includes parks. (Park administrators blatantly pursue a policy of shutting out the homeless through a variety of means: replacing benches on which they can lie down with smaller ones on which they can only sit, removing the roofs from structures that once offered shelter from the rain, cutting down shrubbery, etc.) I believe that it is absolutely essential to come up with the three thousand yen a month it takes to rent a coin locker, the one safe and secure place available for storing things like bedding. I wonder, though, how many of these men actually do this.

In addition to the shanty occupants like Tokunaga and the gnarled, old, bag-toting men who walk the streets, there is one more group of homeless men in San'ya whom I have taken to calling the "rash and reckless."

Unlike the shanty occupants or the bag toters, members of this group do not flinch at placing themselves in full view of ordinary citizens as they go about their daily lives. They don't go around carrying bags; instead, they are always lying down

on their futons, or sitting next to their futons making merry
with their fellow drunks, little realizing, it would seem, that
the bedding is of absolutely no use once it gets rained on.
They appear to be in their cups day and night, but I have no
idea how they get their money for liquor. They are constantly
lighting bonfires in winter, and their faces are always black.

Could it be that these men are in a state of momentary
frenzy—do they go back to the hanba and begin another
round of contract labor once they've sobered up and returned
to their senses? Are they merely seeking temporary respite
from the daily grind by going on a bender for several days
running on the streets of San'ya? I have no idea. But I do
know that this sort of life on the streets cannot possibly last
for long stretches.

Tokunaga and I are both past fifty. Yet we are indifferent to
our situation, notwithstanding the fact that the end of our
tenure in the day labor market is fast approaching. I will
doubtless be excluded from the labor market sooner than
Tokunaga, because I lack his strength and skill. How many
years do I have left? Perhaps only five or six.

During the bubble era, I had a plan, albeit a vague one, for
my old age. My goal was to save enough before the "off-season" to get me by until the time I could go on welfare. And
for a while I indeed worked diligently, calculating the bare
minimum sum of cash I'd need, during this seven- or eight-
year period, to survive on the streets without an income. The
bursting economic bubble and the Heisei recession, however,
smashed my little plan for old age into smithereens.

My becoming a member of the population of truly homeless
seems inevitable, yet this prospect has not exactly chastened
me. I continue to while away the time idly in my bunk, reading books and watching TV with an earphone. Tokunaga,

too, remains indifferent. On the days he can't find work, he goes out on his bicycle and rides about the city, he says. Await the inevitable disaster with equanimity—yes, that is the way to do it. I cannot countenance becoming a parasite at a hanba and being forever ordered about by some young tradesman or site manager, merely for the sake of life's necessities. (I've seen old hangers-on like that working there; my experience at a hanba turns out to have been worth something after all!) I'd much rather become one of the truly homeless, if scavenging for food is all that is required to enjoy the greater part of the day in the library reading books. In fact, I've already made my choice with regard to this issue. Of the two possible visions for the future available to me, I have obviously been avoiding the one that leads to becoming a lifer at a hanba.

Although I can't say for sure, I believe that in the ordinary course of events Tokunaga, too, will perforce descend into the world of the truly homeless. Tokunaga was once a taxi driver, but his license expired long ago, and he will doubtless be facing the same choices as I as he confronts the prospect of old age. He, too, I feel certain, will avoid becoming a lifer at a hanba.

Tokunaga tells me that his shantytown neighbors have virtually nothing to do with each other, and that he himself has exchanged greetings with no one. If you do become friendly with one of your neighbors and then have a falling out, one of you will end up having to move. (He says he's witnessed many such examples.) This way of dealing with people actually is for the better, he says, no matter how unnatural it may appear. My own experience leads me to nod in agreement.

The same thing can be said about one's doya bunkmates. I

suppose it's OK to exchange nods with someone who appears to be a loner, but I think it best to avoid—even to the point of pretending not to notice—the sociable, outgoing sort who keeps trying to make conversation.

Intimate fraternizing among doya bunkmates usually ends in grief. The exceptions, I believe, serve only to prove the general rule. When two men live together in very close quarters, the slightest note of discord between them, having no room to dissipate, cannot but grow more dissonant. If, on the other hand, the two men bearing a grudge go their separate ways, time and distance eventually have their effect and they will forget the grudge. And because a long period of time usually passes before they meet each other again, a feeling of downright nostalgia can well up when they finally do get together, and it's possible for the relationship to commence afresh, as if there had never been a falling out. When the men in question are bunkmates in the same doya, however, there is no opportunity for distance or forgetfulness to take effect. The tiny grudge that they harbor has no chance to diminish, let alone dissipate. The result: bunkmates end up clashing, their grudge swells out of proportion, and one of them is forced to leave the room. I myself have witnessed numerous examples of this.

Here is one such instance.

Gotō-san, an abnormally mild-mannered fellow (I had once thought he wasn't quite all there) with whom I'd worked countless times on jobs arranged through the Center, began lodging in my bunkhouse. He was about the same age as I, but a far more seasoned laborer whose skills were vastly superior to my own. He wasn't the sort who would rub his superiority in your face, moreover; he spoke in deferential language to everyone at the Center and the work site.

I first encountered Gotō in the hallway, and ended up asking his room number. It was then that I learned that he occupied a bunk one room down from me on the other side of the hall. I knew that he was not one to seek the company of others, but perhaps we both had become less cautious. I began visiting his room and chatting with him about work at the Center and about acquaintances we had in common. I didn't think he could possibly be a threat to anyone.

Returning from work one evening, I exited Minami Senju Station to find a sniveling, barefoot Gotō raising hell in front of the newsstand right outside the station. I was speechless. Gotō was blind drunk and didn't even notice me exiting the wicket with my bag over my shoulder; he was too busy hurling the vilest expletives imaginable at the woman tending the newsstand and spitting in her direction. His face tilted slightly upward, he sent his spittle flying at the woman and at the items for sale. As he did so, language I never thought possible from him came pouring out of his mouth: "You rotten cunt!" and so forth. On and on he screamed, in a wild, mean voice.

I was to witness similar scenes with Gotō many times after that. Standing in front of a grocer or hardware shop and drawing himself up into the posture of one of those imposing deities guarding a temple gate, he would spit at the woman inside the shop. His opponent was invariably a woman; his weapon, invariably spittle. At least I never saw him confronting a man, or attacking a woman with anything but his spit.

Gotō continued sleeping in the same bunk one room down and across the hall from me for some time after that first incident (perhaps about three months); I lost all desire, however, to visit him in his room. I'd say hello to him if we met in the hallway, and when I did, he was the same Gotō as always, the one I knew at the Center and at the work site. He'd simply mumble, timidly and with downcast eyes, in response to my greeting. I never learned what became of the spitting incident in front of the newsstand. (Presumably the police became involved.)

Such experiences convinced me of the correctness of Tokunaga's policy of coldheartedness. Put another way, a space permitting the sort of coldhearted behavior that Tokunaga and I engage in is a necessity. Such a space does exist, it would appear, below the expressway in the shantytown where Tokunaga lives (at least to hear him tell it), but not on the terrace right along the riverbank.

To my way of thinking, the possibility that some form of hierarchical relationship would fail to emerge among the men along the terrace who camp out in front of their blue-tarp shanties and drink it up is very slim indeed. It seems far more natural that a class structure (even if not a very strict one) exists among this population of men in their sixties, each group consisting of a kingpin, his inner circle, and his underlings. To prevent infighting among the membership from causing the group to disband altogether—or to stop any infighting to begin with—some form of (semi-)permanent social order becomes necessary. I can think of nothing other than violence, however, that would be capable of producing such a social order among San'ya men.

If it is true that the men who gravitate toward the riverbank terrace must have done so because they could not bear the atmosphere of coldhearted independence that pervades Tokunaga's shantytown, it follows that some form of hierarchy has developed among the terrace occupants. I would not be at all surprised if this population of men living in a hundred or so blue-tarp shacks was comprised of several factions involved in serious rivalry with one another.

Be that as it may, I do not plan to commence my life as a homeless person along the banks of the Sumida River. As I have already explained, I would also not want to live near Tokunaga, in spite of the fact that we get along well enough at present; Tokunaga, for his part, would not, I think, be pleased if I moved next to him, despite our spiritual affinity. At the same time, I have no desire to live in complete isolation from my fellow man. If I am indeed forced into a life of homelessness, I shall envelop myself in some form of collectivity, just as so many others have done. The reason is simple: there is safety in numbers.

Right before coming to San'ya (which is to say about twelve years ago), I lived for a couple of months near Shinjuku Station and got my work out of Takadanobaba. I slept on the lawn adjacent to the large ventilation pipes that are nicknamed "cannon" (I think they're still there) and rise out of the ground near the Keio Department Store at the station's west exit. In that short period I was attacked twice: once right there on the lawn and once when sleeping beneath some shrubbery alongside an office building. The attacks were close together (separated by only a couple of weeks), but I'm pretty sure that the attackers were not the same group of kids each time. Maybe they were the same, but I was convinced, out of an exaggerated sense of danger, that they were not.

The first incident took place, as I said, on the lawn by the "cannon" on an evening in early summer when the weather was just beginning to warm up. It was around eleven o'clock, and five or six kids began hurling rocks at me from the sidewalk on the other side of the street. Glancing in the direction the rocks were coming from, I was amazed at how young these kids were. (They didn't look any older than about twelve or thirteen.) Not to worry, I said to myself, thinking

82

they'd leave soon enough. I relocated to a spot behind another ventilation pipe and tried once more to go to sleep. They were forever moving about, however, shouting "Beggar! Beggar!" all the while and never letting up their rock throwing.[3] When one of the rocks struck my groin, with excruciating result, I rose to my feet to see that they had ventured dangerously close, and I feared for my safety. Hoisting my briefcase to my shoulder and shielding myself with my sleeping bag, I made a run for it. The memory of this first attack remains very vivid in my mind. I was simply astonished by these kids' youth. They must have still been in grade school!

The second attack, two weeks later, took place when I had moved my sleeping spot from the lawn around the "cannon" to a clump of shrubbery alongside an office building. My memory of this attack is not so vivid. Rocks were thrown at me again, but I don't recall any epithets such as "Beggar!" or other abusive language being used. I didn't get a good enough look to determine the culprits' age or number. This time the kids were at some remove from me, beating on the pavement and on the shutters of buildings with a pole or some other long object and trying to frighten me with the noise.

I felt more astonishment and humiliation than fear after being attacked, but I couldn't sleep just the same. In any event, the memory of these assaults led me to conclude that, when sleeping outdoors, it is essential to pick a spot where as many people as possible can congregate.

I don't know how the neighborhood around San'ya compares with, or will compare with in the future, the Shinjuku of twelve years ago in terms of safety. I did hear this one story, however, about a nocturnal attack from a man I'd worked with.

The man in question was a brawny, barrel-chested laborer in his prime; yet one night two middle-school-age boys assaulted him. They had no rocks or poles; instead they kicked him right through his blanket. When the man got up, the two boys ran off in opposite directions, daunted (I would think) by the man's formidable appearance. He chased one of the boys for two or three minutes, but he was no match for a swift-footed middle-schooler, and failed to catch him. This man was sleeping alone, as I had been.

I can't imagine that attacks of this sort occur all that frequently (even though in my case it happened twice within a two-week period). After one has been attacked, however, the fear of another assault disturbs one's repose. A comfortable sleep out in the open, then, requires picking a spot where the possibility of assault by children is virtually zero. That is why people don't sleep alone on the streets.

Once they are old enough to go to high school, boys probably don't even give a thought to attacking homeless men on the street. They have greater obstacles to surmount on the road to establishing their identities. It is the middle-school boys who think of the homeless as hurdles to overcome in the quest to secure their identity, simply because these defenseless men happen to be adults. Twelve years ago, a longtime homeless man in Shinjuku told me that he always got nervous when elementary and middle schools closed down for the longer holidays. The situation very likely hasn't changed.

In addition to children, there lurked one more danger, up until a few years ago, that disturbed one's repose on the streets.

I refer to the frequent outbreaks of crime involving thieves (some working by stealth, some violently) called *mogaki*, who went after laborers returning to San'ya fresh from their jobs at a hanba. By the time these laborers, who had worked for a ten- or fifteen-day stretch, arrived back in San'ya, they were already well in their cups; once here they'd lose all inhibition and drink away until finally they sank, plastered, to the street, with their work bags as pillows. In their pockets were the earnings—ten or fifteen days' worth—that they'd received from their hanba jobs. Men sleeping on the streets in those days were not always dirt poor, as they are today.

Such men would become the targets of *mogaki,* who stole about at night in packs of twos and threes. *Mogaki* would lift valuables from the pockets of men who had passed out drunk; any victim who was awakened by the commotion would first be beaten to a pulp and then robbed. Members of a San'ya labor union formed by radicals used to band up and go on patrol late at night in order to lend a hand to potential victims.

One morning I saw a man who had been nabbed by the union vigilantes and forced to sit on his knees in formal posture on the pavement in front of the Tamahime Employment Agency, with a signboard slung around his neck reading: "I am a *mogaki.*" It was reminiscent of the Great Cultural Revolution in China, a time when government leaders were publicly condemned by ad hoc groups. The man's eyes were swollen and dark red, and blood trickled from his mouth and nose, but he was unable to wipe the blood away because his hands were tied behind his back. He looked young, and was probably still in his early thirties. I don't know if the union vigilantes ever turned him over to the police—their sworn enemy—after that. At any rate, it was a very strange sight.

Mogaki no longer roam the streets of a now lifeless San'ya; the homeless here have nothing to worry about, from them, at least.

About once a month, the promenade along the Sumida River where I walk overflows with pieces of dismantled shanties along with various household effects. Officials from the Tokyo metropolitan government's Park Bureau and the Welfare Office, accompanied by police, make their rounds, requesting those living on the terrace to vacate their shacks. A few days before they make their rounds, flyers announcing the order to vacate are put up here and there; on the day before, shanty residents help each other hoist their dismantled shacks and their contents with ropes, piece by piece, over a concrete dike from the terrace to the promenade. Then, for just a few hours, the terrace is turned over to officials.

As soon as the cleanup operation is over and the officials have left, the blue-tarp shanties are reassembled and restored to their original sites. I am not sure exactly when during my walking career (of five years) this monthly ritual got started. I do recall, however, that the promenade did not fill up with pieces of the dismantled shanties when I began taking walks, so the practice must have started afterward.

Sometimes I veer off my usual course and venture into Sumida Park, where I see men lying about on just sheets of cardboard (although I do spy a few shacks), with everything they own—stuffed in shoulder-strap bags and paper sacks with handles—laid out at their sides. These men, who move about with all their belongings in tow, clearly belong to that previously mentioned population of homeless who are "equally dark of skin and mood." A few of them pile up all their belongings in baby strollers and cart them around that way. If my walk is a bit later than usual, I see many of them getting ready to bed down here and there in the park. These men seem distinctly older than the men living in the blue-tarp shacks along the river.

Twice during the year the Sumida River promenade overflows with people: in spring, during the cherry blossom season, and in late July, on the day that fireworks are set off over the river. Huge crowds gather for the fireworks, and I abstain from my walk on this one day. The crowds during the ten-day cherry blossom season are appreciable, but not large enough to stop me from taking my walks. I simply alter my course a bit.

Last year, while wending my way through the blossom-viewing crowds, I spotted Deguchi-san—a man with whom I'd often ridden a bus to various Tokyo metropolitan government–sponsored work sites and with whom I frequently chatted—scavenging for food in a large trash can put out for the crowds. I pretended not to notice and started to walk by him, but he called out to me. "There are some great box lunches to be had during the cherry blossom season," he said. "Of course," he added, "it's all over when you've fallen this low!" And yet he did not seem particularly disconcerted at having been spotted by me.

Deguchi is in his midfifties. By his own assertion, he used to be a long-distance truck driver, but in the four or five years I've known him, he's never done a lick of work, as far as I can tell, except for those easy jobs hired out by the Tokyo metropolitan government. It didn't look as though he were new to the scavenging business. He is not, however, one of those men who carries his belongings around with him wherever he goes. I am certain that he has built a shack somewhere, but I have no idea where, nor do I intend to find out.

The fun thing about chatting with him is his long-standing interest in sumo wrestling. Our conversations on this topic become very lively. Being able to talk with someone who knows wrestlers like Iwakaze, Tochihikari, and Annenyama is simply a lot of fun. Neither Deguchi nor I are lowbrow fans who go gaga over the likes of the brothers Wakanohana and

Takanohana, grand champions both, or the up-and-coming Chiyotaikai.

We would analyze the difficulties besetting Kotonowaka, who was supposed to share the sumo world's limelight with Takanohana; we'd lament Kyokutenhō's inability to move up in the standings; we'd speculate on the extent of Wakanosato's career-threatening injury. We were agreed that both Kaiō and Musōyama had missed their opportunity to advance to *ōzeki*.[4] (In fact, both were promoted afterward.) We worried that Tochiazuma would end up a mediocre wrestler were he unable to get promoted to *ōzeki* by his midtwenties.

And what about the recent decline in the sport's more colorful aspects?

"The only wrestlers nowadays who will try to lift each other up (*tsuriai*) from a grappling position are Mainoumi and Tomonohana."

"No one throws his opponent with a reverse lift at the edge of the ring (*utchari*) anymore. And no one uses an outside leg hook (*sotogake*) to trip his opponent. You don't see the inside leg hook (*uchigake*) that often, either."

"You're right. And the same goes for the ankle kick (*nimaigeri*) and the backhand throw (*kirikaeshi*)."

"Then there was the judo throw (*yaguranage*). Remember the second Tamanoumi—the one who wore the golden belt? He could pull it off. The first Wakanohana was the only one who could topple his opponent from a clinch position (*yobimodoshi*), though."

"Wrestlers these days have just gotten too big, haven't they? They've lost that resilience in their hips and are simply incapable of making those throws."

Neither Deguchi nor I stoop to the level of discussing, say, the infamous Tochinishiki-Ōuchiyama match, which was decided by a neck throw, or the notorious Tochinishiki-Kitanoumi match, in which the judges overturned the ruling of the referee Inosuke, who tearfully refused to acknowledge their decision. These have been taken up repeatedly by the media, and our own fund of knowledge is not so limited that we need fall back on these episodes.

"If you put Kitanoumi⁵ in with the current wrestlers, he would actually be one of the smaller ones, wouldn't he? His weight would be below the average."

"Chiyonoyama and Myōbudani would be positively diminutive by today's standard—at least in terms of weight."

"How much did Narutoumi weigh, anyway—barely 80 kg (175 lbs.), right?"

"What about Ōdachi? His name was synonymous with the word *giant* in his day. But even he'd be just a bit above average among today's wrestlers."

I am a firm believer in conversation as a method of releasing one's frustrations. Our discourse on sumo, because we can really get into it emotionally, has proved a very effective reliever of stress.

Deguchi and I would talk about almost nothing else. Whenever we met, one of us got things going with a comment like, "Now what about Tōki's straight-arm thrust (*tsuki*)—do you think it's really all that powerful?" and the discussion simply took off. Was Deguchi not itching to chat with me about sumo on this occasion, too? Indeed, wasn't his desire to talk about sumo even greater than his embarrassment (or shame) at having been spotted foraging for garbage?

I myself was hoping that it was, of course; and indeed, we ended up spending nearly an hour that day engrossed in a discussion of sumo.

There is a fleeting moment when, upon returning to the doya after a two-hour walk, sitting down on my bunk, flicking the switch to the fluorescent lamp and turning on the TV, I feel a satisfaction akin to having completed a regimen of religious austerities. I suppose it is not as pleasurable as a "runner's high," but when this physiological aspect of satisfaction—a faint, tingling sensation that radiates from my sides and around my back—wells up in me, I think to myself, "Wow, this could become addictive!" This is the best habit I've ever fallen into—of that I am sure. "So I *am* fifty years old. So I *am* a day laborer in San'ya. At least I've managed to brush up against the joy of walking, if only in a small way." That much I feel at liberty to whisper to myself.

chapter 5

I Am Told by a Foreign Migrant Worker That He Feels Sorry for Me

WE CENTER regulars cast a jaundiced eye on foreign migrant workers. Formerly, I spied many a group of young men on the streets of San'ya early in the morning in search of work and, hearing them talk, realized that, just as I had suspected, they were not Japanese. Even then they didn't venture near the Center recruiting office. The Center issues registration cards that the applicants fill out themselves, but it would never go so far as to issue cards to men one could tell at a glance were foreigners. As for the young men themselves, most of whom came from abroad to work illegally, they were probably afraid to approach the Center, which is a quasi-governmental institution.

Be that as it may, meeting up with foreign workers at a work site to which you'd been dispatched by the Center is no longer the rarity that it was as recently as eight or nine years ago. These days the construction site manager who orders us day laborers around might well be a man with darker skin than a Japanese, and no one will be surprised anymore at finding still other foreigners among the ranks of skilled laborers who install reinforced iron, build concrete molds, plaster walls, and pour cement.

After the economy plunged into recession, however, the idea that foreigners were stealing jobs that belonged to us Japanese began taking root, and the Center regulars' opinion of migrant workers grew even less sanguine. We knew how well the migrant workers' families could live in their native lands even when the workers sent home just half their wages (which were somewhat lower than ours); none of us looked on these foreign youths as particularly gallant or pathetic or otherwise deserving of our sympathy. For their part, they very quickly became aware of our position in Japanese society, and some of them gazed at us in obvious contempt. And while there may be no contempt in the phrase "I feel sorry for you," it's hard to feel good about such words being addressed to you, either.

Four or five years ago I was asked by one work site manager to make the "direct commute" (as we day laborers say) to a job that I had originally obtained through the Center. I did this for about ten days running. Two Koreans, one about fifty and the other in his midtwenties, were working there, and they would chat with me in their broken Japanese during rest periods and the noon break. I couldn't figure out their relationship. That they were not parent and child was obvious enough. I decided that they were two men of differing ages who just happened to be getting work, illegally (or so I surmised), with the same firm. That peculiar rule in Korean society of deference by the junior party to the senior (something I learned from my reading), which would have applied had they been acquaintances from the same village and come to work in Japan together, was not in effect between them. If the older man were indeed fifty, he would have been just a couple of years older than I, yet he had a commanding presence that made him seem for all the world like my father. When I got to talking with him, I realized that he was a fervent patriot. Somehow I was not surprised. He said his name was Shin.

"We go ahead of Japan. This I am sure. Less than ten years." These are the kinds of things he liked to say. The younger Korean appeared to be uninterested in talk of this sort and simply wolfed down his boxed lunch. For ten days I teamed up with this Korean duo and took orders along with them from the site manager. The older Korean assumed the role of team leader and told us what to do. He was far more proficient at Japanese than his young compatriot, and it was possible to carry on an extensive conversation with him.

"I am not man who works like this. I was company president. Do you understand? My company closed. I was forced to come to Japan and earn money." As he spoke, Kim, the younger Korean, would look on with an ironic smile without really listening. (He rarely spoke a word; indeed, it's possible that he understood no Japanese.) Kim did not have the face of an educated person—that much was certain.

"I have three children," Shin said. "Oldest one in college. —— University. You know it?" When I shook my head, he continued, "Good school. He join elite. Give orders. We three here take orders. This is difficult thing."

Shin may have had a problem with Japanese at the level of nuance, not being able to inflect his emotions correctly, but his very direct and open manner of expressing his desire to advance in the world definitely got my attention.

Shin asked me how old I was and learned that I was a bachelor and living alone. "You have no family at your age?" he proclaimed haughtily. "That shameful! You should not tell it to others. I feel sorry for you."

Sometimes I would get into arguments with Shin.

"Japanese not apologize for things they did to us. This no good. One day maybe we attack Japan. But we not do to you what you do to us. We are moral people. We are most moral and most superior people in Asia. This I am sure."

"Oh, really? Then tell me, Mr. Shin. . . ."

I drew the characters for "Chŏlla Province" on the ground and showed them to him.[1]

"Why do Koreans discriminate mightily against people from Chŏlla?" I said, going on the attack. "Japanese don't discriminate against people, say, from the Hokuriku district. How can such a moral people harbor such prejudice?"

I really can't remember exactly how Shin weighed in on the problem of discrimination against the people of Chŏlla, because he always managed to steer the argument toward the problem of Japanese discrimination against Koreans living in Japan, right on cue, as if he were playing the game *Password*.[2] If it happened once it happened a thousand times: the "Korean problem" would be dragged out of the closet. (It was as though time had been frozen at the war's end, fifty years ago.) Utterly vexed, I would argue that Japanese and Koreans had a comparable degree of morality in that both peoples were equally capable of discrimination; Shin, meanwhile, would proudly make his case for the moral superiority of Koreans over Japanese and indeed all Asians, even going so far as to suggest that they were a chosen people.

"Japan number one in Asia now. Korea number two. Some day Korea number one." The hierarchy featured in these pronouncements appeared to have nothing to do with morality, however, and everything to do with economic and political power in the global pecking order.

"That's not true at all," I countered. "China's number one in Asia now, if you ask me."

Shin immediately shook his head. "No, very wrong—very wrong!" he snapped, curling his lips in contempt of China. "Look at Chinese. They fall behind. Long ago they were teacher. Now they are backward country. Their income less than one tenth of Koreans. That country is lowest country. It is dirty country."

"But wait, Mr. Shin," I countered. "Japan and Korea might as well be American colonies. But China's an honest-to-goodness independent nation, isn't it? It has its own nuclear weapons. What other country in Asia besides China can face up to the United States on its own?"

Shin reacted violently to the word *colonies*. "Are you communist?" he shouted. "Korea not colony! United States defend us from attack by North. That is all. How can colony host Olympic Games?[3] People despise you if you say that. Don't talk like communist!"

And so I learned that not only was Shin a stalwart anticommunist, he also had no love, as I'd heard most Koreans had, for China, the country that Korea once recognized as its master.

While at work, Shin and Kim were always at loggerheads. The way they intoned their words in Korean when shouting at each other seemed positively ferocious to my ears, and I would eye them anxiously, wondering what would happen next. After giving each other the silent treatment for all of about thirty minutes, however, they'd be chatting away again in a normal tone of voice. I couldn't help admiring how quickly calm was restored after they'd heaped such abuse on each other.

Elsewhere, at a demolition site, an African (from Ghana) who was operating some heavy equipment once bellowed at me, "Hey, you slowpoke! Hurry up and get to work!" Yes, the gaze that we San'ya day laborers cast on foreign workers is a jaundiced one, indeed.

San'ya is what you might call a mecca for Christian volunteers in the Tokyo area. A hodgepodge of groups representing
several different denominations, Protestant and Catholic,
gather here and engage in a wide variety of relief activities. In
the evening, San'ya men (the ones "equally dark of skin and
mood") will sometimes line up in front of one particular building, which looks like an ordinary house but bears a sign identifying it as the "Church of ———." If you go to the front of the
line you'll notice several young men and women, no doubt
members of the faith, standing in front of a large cauldron and
next to some cardboard boxes filled with Styrofoam bowls.

Soup lines like this one have sprung up not just in San'ya
proper but also in Sumida Park and the open area beneath the
expressway where I take my walks. At some of them you are
forced to sing hymns and join in prayers. I have stood in these
lines a few times myself, but I've decided that it isn't worth a
second trip to venues where hymns and prayers are an obliga-
tory part of the meal.

Among the Christian activists is a middle-aged woman who
is something of a celebrity and who has appeared several
times on TV. Facing the line of men who are waiting for their
food, she does more than spread the Good Word; she delivers
an out-and-out sermon. I am told that any men who do not
respond with the right attitude (such as those who are drunk
or use foul language) she will fearlessly slap across the face
and banish from the premises. I really can't pass judgment on
the behavior of this famous Christian grandma, who is a veritable institution, without first paying a visit to her lair and
witnessing her in action. (It's possible that hers is not at all the
morally putrid act it would appear to be at first blush, but in

fact a lovely, heartwarming episode drenched in humanity.) Given the gist of the stories I've heard, however, I feel only a deep loathing. What I sense from such people's "good deeds" (what Christians call putting their love into practice) is utter shamelessness, and I can't help feeling repulsed.

These Christian volunteers depend in a far more profound way on San'ya men—as objects for their "good deeds" (that is, relief work)—than San'ya men do on the volunteers, yet the famous grandma and her ilk seem all too oblivious to this fact. If, for example, the government were to conduct relief work on a wider scale, San'ya men would no longer need these people; the volunteers, on the other hand, will always require San'ya men as their very own "needy" and as living proof of their own spiritual redemption.

The fact that these volunteers seem to feel no shame at the hypocrisy of their "good deeds" is, I believe, a huge failing on their part. Isn't their obliviousness to this fact the reason they are regarded as complete outsiders here in San'ya?

Like the Christian volunteers, the labor union activists here were originally outsiders who moved into San'ya with political ambitions. They appear, however, to have settled in much more easily and put down far deeper roots than their missionary counterparts. The reason is that these activists, outsiders though they once may have been, now work in the construction industry as day laborers themselves; conversely, some San'ya day laborers take part in union activities.

The union's top leadership is no doubt made up of former students and others among the intelligentsia, but they, too, have grown old, and now it's getting harder to tell who is the former student and who the original day laborer.

As I wait in front of the Center gate early in the morning, activists arrive and distribute leaflets. The leaflets feature propaganda that I can in no way support ("Japanese Empire Maneuvering toward War!" "Japan Bent on Reinvading Korea!"—Do these people live in a dream world?), yet I can't suppress my admiration for the noble bearing of those who are handing them out. When it gets lighter, one of the activists produces a metal table, places it on the street in front of the Center, and plops himself down in a chair behind it, ready to consult with men about their work.

Formerly, hanba bosses accused of wrongdoing by the laborers during these consultations would be asked to attend denunciation sessions held right there on the street. This was a frequent occurrence. The union was backed up by a radical umbrella organization and supported by a group of intellectuals on the outside; together they formed a very powerful political network. No mere hanba boss was a match for the likes of them.

Before calling in the bosses, the union leadership would have already negotiated with the general contractors in charge of the construction sites where the bosses worked; the orders to appear before the denunciation sessions came from the contractors. If that weren't the case, the bosses would never have shown up. At it was, they were resigned to their fate, and the sessions had the feel of a "people's court."

Typically the impetus for these denunciations was the nonpayment of wages and other breaches of contract. Day laborers would rush to the union and complain whenever they felt that they had been shortchanged. (That there are indeed hanba bosses wholly deserving of such denunciations is something I can attest to from my own experience.) The bosses thus had their backs to the wall, having essentially been told by the contractors to bow to the inevitable. Standing before a crowd of union activists and day laborers, they would lower their eyes and mumble repeated apologies amid a torrent of abuse. I've been told that some bosses actually prostrated themselves before a group, although I have never witnessed such a spectacle myself.

"So you really think what you've done was wrong? How was it wrong, exactly? Tell us again, from the beginning!"

These brazen-faced bosses, who had no breeding or formal education but were brought up rather on audacity and derring-do, would repeat their words of apology, in fits and starts, as if trying to trace over letters on a page.

"We can't hear you! Once more, from the beginning!"

With this command, they would be forced to repeat their apologies yet another time.

Any real (which is to say, monetary) settlement doubtless took place before a denunciation session even began; the session itself, then, served as a kind of ritual through which the union boasted of its authority to the San'ya day laborer masses. The whole purpose of the ritual being to rip the transgressors' egos to shreds, the hanba bosses, be they defiant or humble, would not be released until their egos were, in the activists' eyes, sufficiently rent.

These denunciation sessions haven't been held now for several years. Not a few Center regulars believe that construction firms have stopped recruiting laborers from San'ya because they've become gun-shy over just this kind of union tactic.

During the interval between 6:30 a.m., when day laborer recruiting at the Center ends, and 6:45 a.m., when it commences at the Tamahime Employment Agency, union activists will hoist their banner and march from one agency to the other, about a ten-minute walk away. Some thirty activists, spouting political slogans of all sorts, proceed down San'ya's main street, followed by an equal number of plainclothes police armed with walkie-talkies and cameras a short distance behind.

The procession arrives at the employment agency while recruiting is in full swing. When the recruiting winds down, collection of white cards from day laborers eligible for the dole begins. Now the activists turn their loudspeakers on the agency officials, who are busying themselves at their various tasks, and launch protests against the manner in which they do their jobs. This done, the activists once again hoist their banner and march back the way they came, spouting the same slogans in a rhythmical chant. And, just as they did earlier, the plainclothes police follow in their wake.

One more union activity is a common sight for the ordinary day laborer: the weekly soup line that serves either rice-and-miso porridge or dumpling stew. The union soup line is the biggest of all the ones to be found in San'ya, I think. Every Sunday evening, a huge crowd of San'ya men (at least four or five hundred, maybe more), circle the Center in a long line waiting for food. And the volunteers who turn out for this event must number more than twenty.

It is not apparent to the common day laborer what other activities the union engages in; if the leaflets they pass out are to be believed, however, they are involved as well in the ongoing dispute over Tokyo International Airport in Narita, a cause célèbre among radical activists.[4] Once in a while we read leaflets on which are printed scathing condemnations of a rival faction within the union. Although history may deem them outsiders, it is the union activists who in fact rule the streets. (San'ya, too, has its *yakuza* gang headquarters, but the yakuza are not necessarily the principal actors here.[5]) The vet-

erans among them comport themselves in a manner befitting
the true San'ya day laborer. The union even serves as a kind
of private police force; there are some among us day laborers
who, when a serious dispute arises, will take their case to the
union for arbitration. Their political views notwithstanding,
the union activists are, I must confess, an admirable bunch.

I have a chronic disorder of the autonomic nervous system,
and ever since my move into San'ya I've been paying regular
visits to a clinic located in the same building as the recruiting
office. The clinic (officially, the San'ya Welfare Center, a non-
profit organization) is not run directly by the Tokyo metropolitan government. The latter does seem to be involved in its operations, however, and the doctors who are sent there work at
public hospitals in the Tokyo area. The clinic receives patients
three times a day: at 9:30 a.m., 1:00 p.m., and 3:00 p.m. At
any of these times one lines up in front of the window, sub-
mits a form with the necessary information filled in, and then
waits one's turn.

Here one is treated like a child by the doctors, nurses, and
staff. I suppose there is no help for that. Our position in society, after all, is similar to that of children (we don't even pay
for our treatment), so we are left to deliver flawless perfor-
mances as incompetents who might as well be children in the
eyes of society. There is no sense, of course, in flailing about
madly just because our dignity has been trampled on. Many
men, however, do feel that their dignity has been trampled on
at the clinic, and so it is a rare day that one pays a visit and
does *not* witness men hurling abuse at the staff.

I have received medical examinations in complete silence
on numerous occasions here. The doctor would utter nary a

word during the entire exam. Admittedly, only one doctor—a
small, white-haired man who looked to be in his midsixties—
carried out this practice. Sometimes he did not speak to me at
all, from the time I was led into the exam room by the nurse
until the time I left a few minutes later. He didn't stop writing
in his file even when I sat in the chair right in front of him. I
waited for the exam to begin, but he didn't stop writing even
then, so finally, unable to bear the silence, I launched into a
catalog of my symptoms. The doctor still didn't lay eyes on
me, however; he simply continued scribbling in his file. He
seemed to realize that I'd been talking only when I had fin-
ished, at which point he whispered something to the nurse
standing next to him. She escorted me out of the room to an
area where I could take my blood pressure and produce a
urine sample. When I returned with a paper cup and a slip
with my blood pressure recorded on it and handed them to
the nurse, she disappeared with them into the exam room.
Later, when she finally called me back into the room, there he
was, with his nose still in a file. At this point the form he was
filling out seemed to be on my behalf; he handed the completed form to the nurse. "That's all now; we'll get you your
medicine," she said, and ushered me out of the room. During
the entire exam, the doctor did not look at me or speak to me
even once.

I paid this doctor more than ten visits altogether, with virtually the same scenario playing itself out every time. On
some occasions he would deign to gaze in my direction, but
never with a mind to offering a greeting, such as "What's
wrong?" or "How have you been since you were here last?"
I always had to take the initiative, because he didn't ask a
single question. And so I'd begin describing my complaint to
him out of a compulsion to break the silence. He listened all

the while, staring at me blankly, but uttered not a word. When no tests were indicated, he handed the file he had been writing in to the nurse, and the examination came to an end. During the entire session he said nothing to me; nor did he respond to anything I had said. He did not lay a hand on me even once. It sounds preposterous, but it is the truth.

In the end I found out which days this doctor put in an appearance at the clinic and made it a point not to go on those days. I could tell that my patience was in danger of reaching the breaking point. For the last four or five years, I have been able to avoid the torment of putting up with his exams. The exams given by other doctors dispatched to the clinic are really no different from the ones performed by any ordinary physician. They ask questions, they answer my questions, they palpate me. To this day I can't help wondering what on earth that small, white-haired man and his exams were all about.

I have often witnessed day laborers hurling abuse at Center officials who were attending them, both in the recruiting office and in the clinic upstairs. Alcohol has played its role, of course, in pumping up their egos. San'ya day laborers, who aren't blessed with a great many opponents on whom they can test their inflated egos, use the opportunity of their visits to clinic and recruiting-office officials to embark on their fledgling enterprise of ego boosting.

I have also frequently witnessed high-spirited drunks mouthing off at the uniformed officers standing in front of the Mammoth police box.[6] Rumor has it that when the police have had enough talk, they drag the man into the exercise room and practice their judo throws on him, but I have no way of ascertaining the truth of this.

I hear as well that officials in all the San'ya bureaucracies
who have day laborers as clients are prohibited from walking
the streets here on their own, because of the ill will borne
them by the day laborers, but once again, I have no way to
verify this.

Of all those working in San'ya's various bureaucracies, it is
undoubtedly the young clerks at the Tamahime Employment
Agency who are most despised by day laborers. (Their only
rival is the police, who are probably the group most hated by
the union activists.) That they do not go out on their own
surely has to do with various rumors being circulated about
them, and there is every reason to believe that these rumors
have substance.

They are the ones, after all, who stand before a San'ya day
laborer and pass judgment on the authenticity of those
twenty-six unemployment insurance stamps pasted on his
white card over a two-month period—stamps that he cannot
keep out of his mind even in his dreams. Even if he has qualified for the dole by collecting all twenty-six stamps, has duti-
fully turned in his white card by 7:30 a.m., and has then lined
up in at the employment agency window at 1:00 p.m. to receive payment, as protocol demands, he still cannot rest easy.
There is always the chance that, just as he is about to take his
folded card at the window with 7,500 yen sandwiched inside,
he'll be told by a clerk, "Mr. ——, step inside around back."

This is what is known as "the interview." If you get called
in for one, you should understand that your fate for that
month more or less hangs on the result. The employment
agency clerks may be young, but they are trained profession-
als; they have an eye—and a nose—for a fishy-smelling stamp.
Usually they call a man in after something has prompted them
to investigate his case beforehand. They work over the man

104

(who may be as old as their father or even grandfather) like seasoned detectives, browbeating, bluffing, and generally putting the screws on him.

I myself have been called in twice. The first time the clerks had guessed wrong, but even so, they didn't let me out of their clutches for the longest time. Once they had learned that the suspicious-looking stamps were in fact genuine after they checked with the firm that had hired me, they grilled me about every other stamp on the card, scrutinizing my countenance all the while. Admittedly I've never met the real thing, but I must say they went about their business like the vice squad working a criminal case.

The second time I was called in I had in fact used stamps obtained on the black market,[7] and I immediately owned up to my misdeed. I wrote down a pro forma confession as requested and signed my name to it. Because it was my first infraction, I got off with just a two-month suspension of my white card privilege.

This, in a nutshell, is why San'ya day laborers have harbored such deep resentment against the employment agency clerks. It may not be logical, but whenever a day laborer goes through the kind of experience I describe above, he'll ask himself, "Why me?" Or he may think, "But it's just these two stamps out of twenty-six, isn't it?" Yet this line of thought will not win any debates, either. "Here I've managed to get all but two of the stamps needed," he may reason, "and during a recession, too, when there's so little work—even getting up at two or three o'clock in the morning. What's the big deal about just two stamps?" The men cannot hide their frustration. But most of all, they feel a deep sense of indignation at being called in for "the interview" and being grilled by the clerks, and putting up with all the browbeating and bluffing.

Although I can't be sure of it, I'm guessing that this is the
reason why nearly everyone who works for the employment
agency, except for the managerial staff, is rotated after just a
year. Every April,[8] we are greeted by a new slate of faces.

It sometimes happens that a day laborer, while biding his
time in front of the Center waiting for work, gets to chatting
with someone and carelessly lets on that he has a few illegal
stamps pasted in his white card; whereupon his partner in
conversation turns around and reports him anonymously to
the employment agency. The man is exposed, and there ensues
a very dismal scene involving the stamps. The man has no
way of proving that the person he talked to actually ratted on
him, and so the resentment he feels toward his betrayer, too,
ends up being projected onto the agency. There is simply none
among the bureaucrats working in San'ya who is the object of
such deep dislike as these young clerks.

I don't know about Kamagasaki, but there is one crime that
is never committed here in San'ya. The crime in question, as
strange as it may sound, is assaults on women (that is, rape).
This fact can be appreciated if you consider, as I noted earlier,
the aging of the day laborer population and—more important—a passionate interest in gambling that surpasses any interest in sex. Murders are not as frequent as San'ya's image
would have one believe, but one does hear reports of them
from time to time. Perhaps San'ya's most common crimes are
those involving bodily harm; unless the injuries sustained are
serious, however, they aren't reported to the police and so
never become cases to be investigated.

Once in the middle of the day about two years ago I was on
my way to the toilet in my doya when I saw a man in his mid-

fifties marching toward me right down the center of the hallway, thrusting his squared shoulders forward right and left
and glowering at the world all the while. (His exaggerated
posture was like something right out of a cartoon, or like the
histrionic movements of a stand-up comic—so completely unnatural, in other words, that you'd burst out laughing had it
happened anywhere but onstage.) The face of this man, whose
mouth was bent into a crooked scowl, told anyone who was
looking, "OK, which one of you is coming after me?!" The
man glared at me when I hastily stepped aside and curled his
lips as if to say, "You scum!" and then continued to swagger
down the hall in the same histrionic pose.

I returned to my bunk and had been watching TV for about
ten minutes when I heard a loud banging noise; I removed my
earphone and pricked up my ears at the sounds coming from
the hallway.

"What the hell are you talking about? Why do I have to
lend money to someone I've never seen before in my life? Is
your head on straight?"

After these words I heard a dull thud. It was quiet for a
while; then I heard that same loud, banging noise reverberat-
ing from some room farther down the hallway. That, too,
died down and silence returned, but now it had become abnormally quiet; the doya was deathly still. The eerie silence
was broken this time by a clattering noise very close to my
room, followed by a weak protest: "Ah, come off it!" Someone apparently had dialed 110;⁹ the police arrived immediately; and just like that, the man with the swaggering gait was
hauled away. The period during which he had wreaked havoc
in the doya couldn't have lasted more than about four or five
minutes.

After the man was gone, a good many lodgers emerged

from their rooms into the corridor. Their various stories can be summed up as follows. The man, whom virtually no one had even heard of before, went around to each room in the doya and demanded money from whomever happened to be in. He would attack anyone whose answer didn't agree with his expectations, or perhaps it was for some other reason—no one was really sure why—and two men, we found out later, ended up getting hurt. One was attacked while he was in the toilet. Some sort of weapon seems to have been used on him, from the look of the tile-covered walls and floor, which were smeared with blood. "The guy must have been on speed"— this was the general consensus.

It is at times like these that we're forced to recognize the danger of our situation, living in the kind of environment that makes it impossible to be surprised no matter who, among the constant stream of transients flowing into San'ya, ends up becoming one's bunkmate in a doya. After an incident like this, we go to bed wondering what on earth is going through the mind of the man we can hear snoring next to us.

The man occupying the bunk next to mine for four or five months, until about a year ago, was in the habit of talking to himself, and rather loudly, too. His muttering didn't start up until maybe five days after he arrived. Watching a baseball game on TV around seven or eight o'clock at night, he began voicing his opinions on how the game was progressing:

"Come on, Makihara, get a hold of yourself! They're paying you the big salary, aren't they?" Or, "Oh, no—not Kiyohara? You *always* come to bat at a time like this! You'll blow it for sure. I won't get my hopes up. . . . There, see—what did I tell you!"

These were the kinds of things he'd say, in a voice loud enough to overhear quite easily. After a time the man's mutterings strayed from the progress of the game itself to a critique of Nagashima's managerial abilities.[10]

"This team plays a hundred thirty-five games a year, and you are personally responsible for losing ten of them. Ten games in the loss column that the team should have won. Ten games up or down in the standings—you might as well give the other teams a handicap! But the Giants don't have the nerve to fire you, do they? Nagashima, I beg you, for the sake of all Giants fans—just drop dead, will you?!"

I could hear each and every word this man mumbled. A while later he strayed from baseball altogether and broadened his scope.

"Oh, what does it matter? We're all doomed, anyway. The North Koreans are going to fire nuclear warheads right here into the capital of Japan and kill off twenty or thirty million of us.[11] Nobody living in Tokyo is going to survive. I shouldn't worry, though. None of us in San'ya will be around longer than a year or two as it is. It's really sad, when you think about it. They hate us Japanese. It's a missile of revenge. It might be hurtling at us tomorrow. I'm resigned to my death, but those who aren't will be in for a real surprise. Maybe it's better that way, dying without knowing what hit them. . . ."

This was his pet peeve, and I must have heard it dozens of times after that.

One evening, the man came into the room muttering, "I swear, I'll kill that bastard!" And his mutterings continued throughout the evening in the same vein: "If I knock him off in the doya, I'll get caught for sure, so I'll wear a ski mask and do it on the street. Then no one will find out. I'll bet nobody knows I have a dagger and a hatchet. They're all there in my locker: a dagger, a hatchet, an ax—everything! Let's see, now, how to do him in? An ax would leave the biggest gash. . . .

And to think nobody here knows how many times I've mixed it up with the yakuza. I always act innocent and keep a low profile. Nobody has a clue about what kind of man I really am. If they did, their eyes would pop out in amazement. . . . A hatchet would work, too. With a dagger you have to pick your spot carefully, or the fellow isn't going to die. No, it's got to be a hatchet or an ax."

For a long time I was privy only to the man's voice; I never got a look at him in the flesh. One night, however, I happened to cross paths with him at the door to our room, just as he was heading for the main bathing room and dressed only in his underpants and holding a towel and a bar of soap. I realized then and there that he was in fact the respectable sort who could not possibly harm a soul. The instant he set eyes on me, he averted his gaze and walked off. He was a stoop-shouldered, slender-armed, insubstantial-looking man with a paunch for a belly. Looking at the bare back of this rather tall but round-shouldered man who flitted away from me down the hallway, I was convinced that this was not someone schooled in violence.

Most likely, the man talked to himself in order to bolster his self-image. In the end, none of his bunkmates, including me, issued a word of complaint about his muttering, which continued uninterrupted after that. No doubt he wished to impress upon himself and others that he was no mere day laborer on the cusp of old age, but rather a dangerous man, schooled in violence, who could also hold forth on any topic, from baseball to the North Korea problem. Now that he is gone, I have come to realize that the state of mind that produced these mutterings was all too close to my own.

I, too, yearn to impress upon myself and others that I am no mere day laborer on the cusp of old age. The men who lodge in a doya, the men who gather at the Center early in the morning, and even the men who sleep out on the streets—all of them surely yearn for the same thing. And yet, even as they embrace the same hope, they go about their lives managing somehow to control the urge to broadcast it to the rest of the world in the manner of my bunkmate.

I couldn't countenance the facile way in which this man attempted to bolster his mangled ego in the face of life's vicissitudes. That he was a harmless man slightly off his rocker was obvious enough. But crazy people are the sly ones; they don't have to play by the rules.

I am indeed a day laborer on the cusp of old age. And just how shall *I* set about reviving my ego and restoring it to its original state?

chapter 6

I Have Reached the Age
When It Is by No Means
Odd to Take Stock of Life

Ever since I was a boy, I felt that I would never be able to survive in the world of ordinary adults. I always believed in the depths of my heart that I could never lead the life of a normal human being: to go out into society and find a job, to marry a woman and raise a family. Before asking myself whether I even wanted these things, I sensed that this sort of life held no reality for me whatsoever.

I was deeply convinced that I simply wasn't suited for that life. As if to brush aside this conviction, I drove myself excessively for periods of time in an effort to adapt to the ways of society (which is to say, the corporations I worked for). When I finally realized, however, that there was a physiological limit to my ability to conform, I actually felt relieved. *Of course* I can't live out my life in a place like this (that is, in some corporation, or society in general), I told myself with profound satisfaction.

A cousin on my mother's side who was a couple of years older than I, and who looked very much like me when we were children, was hospitalized in a mental institution from the time he was in his twenties. (I believe that he is still confined.) I never made any direct inquiries, but I can surmise that he was institutionalized for depression. That we resembled each other physiologically was clear enough as well; yet for me a life of confinement seemed even more unbearable than life as an ordinary citizen. Was there no way for someone like me, who was incapable of working in a corporation and living in ordinary society, to survive without being put away in an institution? At some point, this worry lodged itself in my brain and wouldn't go away.

I shudder to think of what might have happened to me had there been no social outlet in Japan like Kamagasaki or San'ya. (To put it the other way around, the prospect of a life in Kamagasaki or San'ya really doesn't give me the creeps at all.) Being unable to maintain steady relationships with other people means, of course, being unable to hold down a job; if this were a socialist country, I would undoubtedly have been shipped off to a mental hospital long ago. I count among my good fortunes the fact that Japan never went socialist.

My second good fortune is having been able to live in Japan *after* the high-growth era. No one with my puny physique living before or during that era—to say nothing of before the war—could have made it as a construction worker. And had I been unable to earn a living in construction, I would have had no means of earning a living, period, given my inability to interact with other people on a steady basis. In that case I would have led the life of an incompetent and, perforce, would have been supported by my family. Such a life, I felt, whether in the form of semiconfinement at home or total confinement in an institution, would have been quite unbearable for me. Times have changed, and today people would probably not be so quick to institutionalize social derelicts like myself, but such was not the case during my boyhood and youth—which is to say, the Showa thirties and forties (1955–74). I lived then in constant fear of being placed in confinement. And that is why I felt so driven to adapt to society and to corporate life.

It has been my profound good fortune, then, to live in an advanced capitalist country. One might even say I've had no greater fortune than being able to partake of a few crumbs from the abundant table of postwar Japan. The righteous indignation of a man like Saitō (Mr. "One-Man Salvation Army") is simply unfathomable to me. Saitō is no doubt furious that the world doesn't operate at the optimum level of +100; yet to me, such an attitude is simply arrogant. I for one believe that things are just fine if the world manages to hold the line at about –10. Postwar Japan actually seems to be about +5 or +10, and I honestly cannot comprehend the feelings of those who wish for better than that. Those who do surely must be living under some delusion.

We do not live in a world in which we must choose between (a) +100 and (b) –100. Our actual choice is something closer to that between a –2 and a –5; we can't even determine, moreover, *which* choice is the –2 and which the –5. Or maybe it is in fact a choice between, say, the *red* –3 and the *black* –3. It's a choice, in other words, between two totally different but equally bad things. I am really put off by the simplemindedness of those who insist that ours is a world in which absolute good (+100) butts heads with absolute evil (–100).

The choice I will be making as I face old age is between two very different lifestyles, both with negative values. The first is working at a hanba, leading a dog's life from which there is no escape (and for the sake of which one must constantly maneuver and jockey for position), but which guarantees the daily necessities. The second is a life of scavenging for food which, however, liberates one completely from dealings with other people while allowing one to enjoy such activities as reading in the library. I shall opt for the latter choice without hesitation. Both choices have negative values, but I would rate the former at about a −50, and the latter at only a −10. (A −50 would be for me just about the worst rating imaginable.)

It is easy enough to conjure up the sort of scene that would spark the outrage of someone like the activist Saitō, to wit: a wealthy executive riding in a chauffeured limousine driving by a homeless man foraging garbage from a trash can on the streets somewhere in the metropolis. Were he to witness such a scene, Saitō would be crying out for social justice until he was blue in the face. I, on the other hand, would be thinking about the heavy responsibilities shouldered by that same executive and feel very grateful not to be sitting in his seat. Since I can imagine just how carefree the life of a vagrant is, once he gets used to the idea of people watching him scavenge for his food, I don't think of it as the ultimate tragedy that it is usually made out to be. Most important, a society that exhibits such an obvious gap between rich and poor is also one that tolerates diversity (insofar as it doesn't round up the scavengers and cart them off to an institution). Just what a person considers to be the ultimate misfortune depends on that particular person's values. Thus it is utterly simplistic and jejune to conclude that one's own idea of great misfortune is an absolute misfortune for all. (I would probably have to reserve judgment in the case of certain types of illness, however.)

There are, of course, certain scenes that would engender disgust, if not outrage, even in me. Consider the following: An audience rises to its feet and gives a thunderous ovation to some highly respected leader following his oration, and the applause never dies down. Members of the audience wear expressions of rapt adoration on their faces; the leader himself, in a gesture of apparent self-satisfaction, responds to the ovation with a smiling countenance and a slow, rhythmical clap of the hands.

Saitō and his ilk, unable to contain their outrage at spectacles like this, have no doubt thrown body and soul into the work of eradicating them; whereas I, in my disgust, have wanted only to remove myself from such scenes. Not only do I loathe the idea of being part of them, I yearn to get as far away from them as possible.

As long as those who would idolize other people go about producing these spectacles in a place I cannot lay eyes on, I have no objection. That there are not a few who engage in such pastimes would seem to be one of life's unshakable truths. (There is probably nothing more pleasurable than the feeling of reverence that accompanies cult worship.) I think it useless to denounce such a truth about human existence. Such people have every right, after all, to enjoy their pastime (that is, cult worship) to the hilt. I know full well that members of religious groups in some corner of society or another indeed indulge their pastime and wallow in their guru's authority; I have no objection to any of this as long as it doesn't involve me. The collapse of the socialist fantasy has meant that the fear I had about becoming involved myself in a similarly disgusting spectacle has disappeared. This is something for which I must say I am very grateful.

I judge life according to a very low standard, objectively speaking. That, I suppose, is why I can conclude that mine has been far from the worst of lives, for the simple reason that I've been able to avoid being shipped off to a mental hospital or being kept at home in semiconfinement, and instead have concentrated on looking out just for myself ever since becoming an adult. Because I never had the feeling that I could have lived a life superior to—or different from—the life I actually lived, I was able to accommodate myself quite easily to an existence that, from an objective point of view, is rather miserable. The kind of sentiment that drove a man like Katō, the former radical, to bellow at the heavens, is not to be found in me, at least not at the conscious level.

I have lived a total of fifteen years as a day laborer, three of them in Kamagasaki and twelve of them in San'ya, yet I have never beheld the kind of lofty or beautiful human spirit that people somehow expect to witness at the bottom of society. The human spirit that inhabited the majority of San'ya day laborers, insofar as I could tell from my years living in ordinary society, was neither as lofty nor as beautiful as that to be found in the average citizen. Neither was the baseness of those living in San'ya as multifaceted or as well camouflaged as that of people living in the outside world; indeed, it was far more straightforward and plain. I have lost count of the men I have run across who embody a veritable trinity of ignorance, meanness, and arrogance. No special value should be attached to learning by itself, I suppose, but whenever I brush up against one of these ignorant, mean, arrogant men, the importance of education as a means of acquiring learning is further brought home to me.

I have never met an uneducated man who was able to eradicate his own baseness through strength of character alone. The San'ya day laborers I believed to be possessed of superior character and demeanor (Tsukamoto and Ogata and Tokunaga) were by no means lacking in intellect. Those men who *were* lacking in it seemed, as a rule, to invite meanness and arrogance precisely because of that lack. To wit: an old-timer who lived in my doya, himself on the dole but un-

able to contain himself when walking past a vagrant foraging garbage at a dump site, spat on the ground and blurted
out, "Ugh, you filthy beggar!" This happened right before
my very eyes, and I could barely resist the urge to cuss the
man out. In San'ya, the baseness of human beings has descended to a low level indeed.

Considering the extraordinary—indeed, superhuman—
willpower necessary to prevent ignorance from leading to
baseness and shame, I am tempted to declare unequivocally
that ignorance is the mother of them both. If, on the other
hand, a person possesses willpower so exceptional that it prevents his ignorance from giving birth to either, then it must
mean that he has in fact acquired a modicum of intellect at
some point. Once you come into contact with San'ya men
who embody this trinity of ignorance, baseness, and arrogance, you can't help realizing just how refined the shifty
business of ordinary people—all the guessing games and
backbiting behind a facade of goodwill—actually seems by
comparison.

If the amount of baseness to be found in this world is in
fact offset by an equal amount of nobility, then there ought
to exist somewhere here in San'ya the noble-mindedness to
counterbalance the degree of baseness that one readily finds
among day laborers. Lacking as I am in enterprise and
strength of character, however, I have not been able to locate
it.

I believe that I can detect, in addition to certain ideological
assumptions, the following psychological factor at work in
those who would romanticize the San'ya day laborer—op-
pressed, despised, and discriminated against—on the basis of
that very oppression and discrimination. It is safe to say that
these individuals (intellectuals who get frequent coverage in

the media) are far superior to the ordinary person in terms of intelligence, tenacity, and moral conscience. The same psychological mechanism that enables a holy man to draw out the dormant bit of holiness in anyone he comes into contact with also comes into play when one of these eminent intellectuals encounters a San'ya day laborer and makes the latter experience a high-mindedness that he doesn't ordinarily feel. And when this happens, doesn't he appear in the eyes of these intellectuals as a kind of "noble savage"?

This is the same as saying that it is the very power of these intellectuals' minds and personalities that has awakened the nobility slumbering in the San'ya day laborers' breasts. That is all fine and good, but such an awakening is without question a temporary thing. The day laborers will soon revert to their original baseness. This is what is meant, I think, by the expression "A person too exalted is blind to the character of his fellow man."

During my long career in San'ya, I have tried to reduce to the bare minimum the need for resuscitating my wounded ego by making it a practice to shrink it to the smallest possible dimensions. This is a defense mechanism I acquired quite naturally out of the realization that nothing presents so great a danger to the San'ya day laborer as his attempt to sustain himself on inflated pride. Yet such a mechanism notwithstanding, I am even now beset by an occasional ego crisis, during which I feel the same urge to bolster the pride welling up in me that I suspect must have welled up in the breast of my former bunkmate who was forever talking to himself. Still, I could never have expressed that urge in the form of violence. Even when I was convinced that fighting was the only answer, the vitality that enables one to embark on a violent course never sprang forth in me.

There are dozens of older men living in my doya who are on welfare support from the government. Several of them sport brilliant tattoos on their backs. The stark contrast between the sheer magnificence of those tattoos and the forlorn expressions on the men's faces, however, is pitiful to observe. Must not having to cope with the contradiction that exists between the silent menace that their naked backs pose to others and the meek expressions that their own faces now present to the world add substantially to the burden that these men shoulder in their waning years?

One's true self is that which exists in the gaze of other people. Here in San'ya, I have continually practiced the technique of bringing my inmost self closer to the self that others have come to expect; for someone like me who must live out his days in San'ya, there is nothing more to do in life than refine this technique.

One's needs in life beget one's philosophy. I cannot countenance a religious philosophy that simply goes about balancing the accounts of one's life in this world. I want nothing to do with absolutists who maintain that virtue is rewarded with the blessings of heaven and that evil is punished by the tortures of hell. Isn't this system of retribution itself filled with a kind of relativism?

A commitment to leading all people to salvation, without distinction and without favor, and regardless of the kind of life they have lived in this world—surely this is the mark of the true absolutist. Isn't the true absolutist one who extends the same salvation to all people, no matter how they have lived in this world? This absolutist would lead even Hitler, Pol Pot, and Asahara[1] to salvation, extending the same absolute mercy to them as to all others. It is *precisely* for this reason, however, that we creatures of this world must not forgive the Hitlers or the Pol Pots or the Asaharas. Secular society must be acknowledged for the relativist world that it is and be governed with the strictest impartiality. On the far side of this world, however, another world awaits us, a world of absolute and indiscriminate salvation. This is what I believe, and this is why I revere the absolute being known by the name of Amida Buddha. A world of absolute and indiscriminate salvation should be there, waiting for us all, on the other side of death.

Thus, when it is time to die, I shall place myself at the mercy of this being and declare my faith: *Namu amida butsu.*

author's postscript

Aт the end of July 2003, I moved out of my doya, the one I write about in this book and my home in Tokyo for more than fifteen years, and began living on the streets. The following is an account of what impelled me to leave the San'ya *do-yagai* altogether.

The prize money I received for the manuscript that became this book was a wholly unexpected windfall which provided a substantial boost at a time when my savings account had been shrinking steadily for lack of work. The sum was by no means large enough to eliminate all anxiety about surviving into old age, but it did liberate me for the time being from the necessity of plunging into that mad predawn rush for a job.

And so it was that I abandoned my morning commute to the Center. I was doing my compatriots a favor, I reasoned. Indeed, by absenting myself from the premises I was increasing the odds for everyone else to get work. That was just an excuse, of course. Feeling quite snug in the security of my bolstered savings, I found I no longer had any stomach for the naked struggle that awaited us day laborers morning after early morning.

Anyone who felt as I did about work might indulge in similar reasoning. My dislike of working, however, was born not of some distaste for the physical aspect of labor but rather of my inability to interact with other people.

But now, suddenly, I had come into funds sufficient to allow me not only to feed and shelter myself for an appreciable period but also to avoid all contact with other people. Nothing could have been more appealing to me. Money had given me freedom of a particular kind: the freedom to disassociate myself from my fellow man.

At this point I simply could not bear the thought of arising at the crack of dawn (or, more often than not, in the middle of night), let alone camping out on a piece of cardboard in front of the Center from the previous evening, for the sake of landing a job on the following day.

Ironically, it was only after I won the award and money was deposited into my account that my frugal ways commenced in earnest. For example, I suppose I have reached the age when I should be abandoning any thought of having sex; yet try as I might there are times when the urge is just too great. That doesn't mean I can yield to temptation, however, and simply go out and buy a woman's favors. Whenever I am seized by lust, I have to go it on my own—self-service, if you will. Well and good: any deficiencies in my sex life are a small price to pay for the pleasure of living apart from my fellow man.

In short, my life of thriftiness really began with the receipt of a windfall literary prize. From then on I spent no money whatsoever on anything except food and shelter and did no work except for those easy cleanup jobs doled out by the Tokyo metropolitan government. It was a truly bizarre turn of events.

Thanks to the money in the bank, I realized that I could maintain a certain level of subsistence without doing any work for a considerable period. "Well, then," I told myself, "let's see if I can stretch the days I can subsist to the greatest possible number." Eccentric thought, yes; but this compulsion of mine was not to be denied.

At this stage in life I no longer feel the need to accomplish anything in order to justify my existence; at the same time I appreciate the human need to avoid certain things at all cost in order to survive. I have gone to very great lengths up to now to avoid the frustration and disillusionment that is brought about—inevitably, as far as I am concerned—by the kind of human interaction that accompanies nearly any job. I am convinced, moreover, that I would go to the same lengths all over again if need be.

Now if I were somehow able to avoid having to work altogether, I was confident of being able to tolerate an existence that consisted solely of eating and sleeping—an existence devoid even of conversation with another human being—for weeks on end. (The cleanup work sponsored by the Tokyo metropolitan government is the exception here and needn't be avoided; I think of it as an amusement and not at all as something stressful or burdensome.)

When the time comes to take stock of things, it hardly matters to me if my existence has not been blessed by events that can be put in the "plus" column. I will consider my life a success if I have reduced to the bare minimum—as close to zero as possible—those events that must be relegated to the "minus" column.

In such a frame of mind I had been warily eyeing my

shrinking savings account and calculating the number of extra
days I could subsist if only I were able to eliminate the expense of lodging. Slowly but surely the feeling welled up in me
that the time had come to do just that. I disposed of my substantial accumulation of household effects, made up my bed
thoroughly (I wanted to leave a favorable impression with the
people at the front desk), and left the doya for good, without
informing the management.

If my descent into homelessness was unavoidable, then it
behooved me to ensure that circumstances not take on a tragic
hue. Thanks to the wealth of reading I'd done on the subject
at the local library, I had always felt confident that I could
avoid the slide into the depths of misery that proved to be the
reality of homelessness for so many. And was not money, in
the final analysis, the ultimate safety brake, capable as it was
of stopping the final slide?

So reasoning, I had long ago resolved to embark on the
homeless life voluntarily, with some money still in my pocket
(not literally, of course, but safely deposited in my savings account), that is, long before I had become flat broke and had
been thrown out on the street.

While working on my manuscript, I had the vague notion
that homelessness for me would begin at around the age of
sixty. I am still just fifty-six years old, but perhaps this miscal-
culation falls within the allowable margin of error.

More than a few men who once worked as day laborers out
of San'ya remain there to take up the homeless life even after
they are no longer hirable. I had felt from the beginning, however, that this would not be my way. True, I had entertained
the notion of putting up a shanty like Tokunaga-san's at one
point; but such is the proper course only for those who
choose to continue working as casual laborers while living on

the streets. If I were serious about abandoning my day laboring career entirely, it made no sense to remain in San'ya, or so I reasoned.

It is my conviction that former day laborers linger in San'ya out of a fear of separation from their friends and acquaintances. Happily (for this is how I look at it), I am fettered by no such close relationships. All my interactions with San'ya people, including Tsukamoto-san, have been (and here I'm putting things in the best possible light) as free flowing as water. Abandoning them would be no cause whatsoever for regret.

One more thing—and, speaking as someone new to homelessness and blessed moreover with a modicum of savings, I must offer my comments guardedly: I wonder whether most people living on the streets lack sufficient resolve. They seem rather too quick to rely on the generous welfare resources available to them in San'ya and elsewhere. Not only does the city government provide various services (I am thinking, for example, of the large facility on Ōi Wharf near Tokyo Bay, which provides men with temporary food and shelter), but numerous private organizations also offer soup lines over a sizable area that includes Ueno and Asakusa. I understand that by taking advantage of every soup line available one can get by almost never having to scavenge for food. To my way of thinking, however, the men who choose such a course are deficient in their resolve and, frankly, rather naive.

Anyone who has partaken in these soup lines, I hasten to add, will understand what I mean when I say that the menus are frightfully monotonous and simple to a fault. Meals doled out by the city government consist of bread, margarine, jam, and milk; those by private volunteer groups comprise one or more of the following: rice curry, rice balls wrapped in seaweed, miso-flavored rice porridge, and stewed rice with a side of pickled vegetables. People on a steady diet of either menu may not be underfed, but they will almost certainly end up malnourished.

That is why the most attractive location for a life on the streets is one of the city's busier districts. It is surely far better for someone taking the great plunge into homelessness to leave San'ya behind and head for the crowded termini of Shibuya or Shinjuku, or upscale shopping districts like the Ginza, or fashionable night spots like Akasaka, Aoyama, and Roppongi. There the homeless man can devote himself to the task of securing a diet of high-calorie, protein-rich garbage found in abundance in such locations. Indeed, by doing one's own scavenging, it is no doubt possible to manage one's diet right down to the last vitamin and mineral.

With this plan in mind, I abandoned San'ya for the streets of Shinjuku, and that is where I now live. I have yet to scavenge my meals, however. I am quite able to get by without doing so if I so wish for a long time to come. At the same time, I can feel a desire welling up inside me for the kind of thrill that scavenging would provide. If I were to rummage through the garbage for my meal today, I could then afford to buy a movie ticket. I'd take in one of those American suspense thrillers I like so much. . . . If I look at things in this light, the day I begin scavenging may not be that far off. I have yet to put up any structure for a dwelling.

I was born in 1947, the sixth child in a family of seven brothers and sisters living in western Kagawa Prefecture on the island of Shikoku. I was the fourth son. (Families of this size were not at all uncommon then.) My father worked for himself and tried his hand at several businesses. He ran a

127

newspaper outlet for some years when I was a child; later he opened a branch office of a securities firm. (I believe that he was actually in the firm's employ.)

All my five brothers and sisters (not counting the one who died while still an infant) have their own families and lead normal lives. Two brothers (one was a branch manager of a large bank and the other a middle-ranking executive in a canning firm) are by now retired. I surely have many nieces and nephews, but I've met only one of them, the daughter of my eldest sister. The last time I had any contact with members of my family was when I was thirty-seven, which is to say about two decades ago. I really can't say how much they regard me as a black sheep; what is certain is that I gave up staying in touch with them, and they eventually stopped trying to contact me. By the time I had arrived in San'ya I was no longer informing them of my whereabouts. Each side, clearly, wanted nothing more to do with the other. I certainly did not want to be found by them.

I stated previously that the two brothers who worked at the bank and in the canning firm have now entered into happy retirement; yet this is only speculation on my part. (I do know that my banker brother's son has himself become a branch manager.) I believe that the estrangement from my family I describe here quite typifies the San'ya day laborer's experience. It may well be a classic case.

I remember being an unremarkable and awkward child. Ever since puberty I felt completely ill at ease with myself and with members of the opposite sex. I have never slept with a woman who was not a prostitute. I am, in short, a man with no talents who is incapable of relating to women or coping with work. I do not say this out of self-reproach. On the contrary, I am confident that the self-portrait I offer here is in fact an objective assessment of how people regard me.

author's postscript

Other than gaining entrance into a reasonably good second-tier public university, having my manuscript selected for the Kaikō Takeshi Prize and for subsequent publication is really the only major achievement in my life. I was truly astounded by the news. Never did I dream of such a thing happening to me at the ripe age of fifty-three. I was afraid, however, of acquaintances' learning about this honor, because I simply lacked the energy to fill in the immense gap between this "achievement" and what I knew to be my true character. I could hardly reestablish contact with members of my family simply on account of this development, and so to this day not one of my brothers or sisters knows anything about it. I seriously doubt that anyone who knows me has connected me to the prize. (Any suspicions the staff at my doya may have had about the many articles of mail that arrived at the front desk with my name on them they thankfully kept to themselves. What if they had said something like, "Why, isn't that wonderful?" or, "Wow, that's really some accomplishment!"? How could I have faced them after that?)

The relief I felt when the publisher granted my timid request to absent myself from the award ceremony, about which I had been so terribly anxious, was no less great (albeit an emotion of a different stripe) than the joyous excitement I felt upon being first notified by telephone about receiving the prize. The Ōyama Shirō in real life, after all, was an even more dull-witted and unattractive person than the one who appears in the pages of this book.

All that was more than three years ago. As one who no longer works and who has now abandoned the *doyagai* altogether in favor of a life on the streets, I am no longer qualified to discuss recent trends in San'ya—if, in fact, I ever was. (I was never really a part of San'ya life, especially in my later years there.) I will make note, however, of one recent trend I have observed. A new type of laborer—one very different from the construction worker of yesteryear—has appeared at the Center in the wake of increased job offerings by the city government to offset rising unemployment.

This new laborer—typically an older man of smaller build, whose downcast eyes and frail physique are in stark contrast to the strong and robust if rowdy sort who was such a San'ya fixture in earlier years—has become far more prominent of late. True, such men were around before, but they did not gather at the Center looking for work. The newcomers, who did some day laboring but still lived on the streets, were formerly scattered about the city. They have been drawn to San'ya by rumors of work in public parks of the easy cleanup variety, made available through the Center.

This is the San'ya I left behind to live on the streets—a San'ya that is becoming more and more an old men's town. Never again will I be working like a coolie in jobs that exhaust me from the strain of having to reign in my frustrations even before I taste the strain of actual physical labor. If moving into San'ya amounts to a kind of withdrawal from life, then moving out of San'ya onto the streets signifies, I suppose, the ultimate retreat.

To others I must appear to be leading a rather zombielike existence. Yet even if my present life, which has embarked on a new phase, cannot be called a happy one, the fact that it has become an exceedingly tranquil one, quite as I'd predicted—one which has liberated me from the demons of fear and uncertainty and profound anxiety that had constantly threatened to overwhelm my previous existence—brings me no little satisfaction.

Shinjuku, autumn 2003

notes

chapter 1

1. *Doyagai* means "*doya* (lodging house) district." Doya come in several grades: the more expensive, multistory "business hotel" type, with tiny, air-conditioned, single-occupancy rooms; older, single-occupancy lodging houses without air conditioning; and "bunkhouses" (*beddohausu*), which typically accommodate eight men per room.

2. The Showa [Shōwa] era is the reign name of the emperor Hirohito, who sat on the throne from 1926 to 1989. The Showa era was followed by the Heisei era (1989–), the reign name of the current emperor (Akihito).

3. Work is unavailable during these holidays. Obon, the Buddhist festival of the dead, takes place, with some exceptions, in mid-August.

chapter 2

1. The recruiting office (San'ya Rōdō Sentaa) is run by the Tokyo metropolitan government. The Welfare Center also houses a clinic and other facilities in its four-story building. The recruiting office's lower rate of pay, compared with that of jobs to be had off the street, was offset by the security that came with the municipal government acting as middleman.

2. The sluggish state of Japan's economy continues at the time of this translation. Since the book's publication, injuries of the sort the author describes have prompted Center officials to alter the procedure for lining up.

Now the shutters open *before* the gate does, and the few men still participating in this ritual go directly from the gate to the recruiting office windows.

3. *Hanba* are construction sites, usually away from the city, requiring the services of live-in workers doing "contract" or long-term work. Day laborers can sign up for a term of several weeks or even longer. The income is steady, if low, and living conditions are often very poor.

4. A *tobi* or *tobi shoku,* named after the most common raptor in Japan, is a highly skilled worker who assembles and disassembles scaffolding on buildings. Many work as day laborers.

5. Musashimaru (b. 1971), from Hawaii, became the sixty-seventh *yokozuna* (grand champion) in 1999 and was the top wrestler at the time Ōyama wrote his book. Futabayama (1912–68), the thirty-fifth *yokozuna,* whose wrestling career stretched from 1927 to 1945, still holds the record for the longest winning streak, sixty-nine matches in a row.

6. The recently retired Terao (b. 1963), who wrestled in the Makuuchi division (the highest level) during the late 1980s and 1990s, compensated for his relatively light weight (250 pounds) with very agile movements.

7. Tochigiyama (1892–1959) and Tamanishiki (1903–38) are the twenty-seventh and thirty-second *yokozunas,* respectively.

chapter 3

1. Hieizan, the general term for a complex of temples founded in the ninth century atop Mount Hiei, overlooking Kyoto, the old capital, is one of the largest and most important Buddhist compounds in Japan, and the headquarters of the Tendai sect. In the early middle ages, it was the home of priests who occasionally descended the mountain to assert their will violently on court politics.

2. "White cards" (*shirotechō*) are issued for the purpose of verifying work performed by day laborers that qualifies for credit toward unemployment compensation. The Tamahime Employment Agency and the Center recruiting office are the two municipal hiring agencies in San'ya.

3. A high plain on the northwestern flank of Mount Fuji, a dozen miles from the summit.

4. Nagashima Shigeo (a star infielder with the Yomiuri Giants), Oh Sadaharu (a star outfielder with the Giants), and Inao Kazuhisa (a star

pitcher with the now defunct Nishitetsu Lions), were among the best-known players of their day. Their careers, lasting from the late 1950s to the early 1970s, paralleled the high-growth era.

5. Asaka Yui (b. 1969) is a well-known pop singer, although not a superstar.

6. The author mentions elections in apparent reference to the Kōmeitō, the political wing of the Sōka Gakkai, a broadly popular and vigorously evangelical religious sect that is the object of the author's venom here.

7. A small *yoseba* is located near Takadanobaba, two stations north of Shinjuku on the Yamanote Loop Line. Unlike San'ya, it has no *doyagai*, and day laborers commute to the site from places like Shinjuku.

8. The Jōban Line connects the northeast suburbs of Tokyo and beyond with Ueno, a major terminal on the Yamanote Loop Line. Minami Senju, one of the stops, is in San'ya.

9. Part of a mountain range located on the western edge of the Kantō Plain about thirty miles from the center of Tokyo, it is still a relatively wild and remote area.

10. A subway station on the Hibiya Line, in central Tokyo.

11. A district in Ōta Ward, in south Tokyo, the opposite end of the city from San'ya.

chapter 4

1. The onomatopoeic *pachinko* is the name of an extremely popular form of pinball game. Winners exchange the small metal balls they have won for prizes like cigarettes and chocolate; they can then exchange their prizes for cash, if they wish, outside the *pachinko* parlor at a special booth. The two-step process of making money off the game is the technical loophole that prevents it from being categorized as a gambling activity.

2. Men are recruited for work in the order of their white card registration numbers, and those making themselves available for the "special jobs" sponsored by the Tokyo metropolitan government would be on call, so to speak, for a month.

3. "Beggar" (*kojiki*) is a particularly stinging epithet in Japanese, because the word's connotations of "outcaste" linger in the cultural memory.

4. *Ōzeki* (champion) is the second highest ranking after *yokozuna* (grand champion).

5. A *yokozuna* whose heyday was in the mid-1980s. Not the same wrestler as the previously mentioned Kitanoumi.

chapter 5

1. One of the three major regions of South Korea, located in the southwest, Chŏlla has been the site of many uprisings against central government rule over the years, including one in the capital of Kwangju in 1980 which resulted in an infamous massacre perpetrated by government troops.

2. The author uses the name of a popular and long-running Japanese TV game show (*Rensō geemu*); the equivalent American TV game show from the 1970s is used here.

3. Shin is referring to the Summer Olympics held in Seoul in 1988.

4. In the late 1960s, student radicals teamed up with local farmers in Narita, some forty miles from downtown Tokyo, and began protesting the government's seizure of farmland for use as an international airport, delaying the airport's opening until 1978 with just one of three planned runways. The protests have continued, and the second runway was opened only in 2002.

5. This is not to say, however, that *yakuza*, or Japanese Mafia, play a minor role in the life of day laborers. Through their network of street agents, they have a virtual monopoly on job offerings on the street corners (as opposed to places like the Center recruiting office and the Tamahime Employment Agency), as well as on the black market for unemployment insurance stamps. They are also heavily involved in gambling operations in San'ya.

6. This San'ya institution (named for its size), which has a checkered history and which has been relocated at least twice, now stands on the west side of San'ya's main street. It is the principal police presence in the area.

7. Historically, there has been a flourishing black market for the stamps, controlled by *yakuza*, with the price of stamps rising and falling with the availability of jobs. The going rate at the time of this book's publication was about 1,000 yen, which of course was seen as an investment in the 7,500 yen unemployment dole one would receive for up to nearly half the days in a two-month period if one was successful at collecting all twenty-six stamps during the previous two-month period.

8. The fiscal year in Japan begins on April 1.

9. The direct telephone line to the police anywhere in Japan; something like the 911 number in the United States.

10. Formerly a star third baseman for the Yomiuri Giants and perhaps Japan's most popular player of all time, Nagashima Shigeo was the team's manager at the time this book was written. Makihara (a pitcher) and Kiyohara (an outfielder) were players on the Giants' team.

11. The reference here is probably to the August 1998 incident in which North Korea fired a missile into the waters off the coast of Japan, causing a stir.

chapter 6

1. Asahara Shōkō (real name Matsumoto Chizuo), the former leader of a religious cult known as Aum Shinrikyō (Aum [Om] Supreme Truth; now renamed Aleph), was tried and later convicted of masterminding the lethal sarin gas attacks (among other sensational mass murders) on Tokyo's subways in March 1995.

suggested readings

A SMALL but growing body of literature exists in English on casual labor in Japan. I shall limit myself here to book-length publications on the subject. My *San'ya Blues: Laboring Life in Contemporary Tokyo* (Ithaca: Cornell University Press, 1996) provides a general description of Tokyo's largest day laborer community as it was during the bubble period, which ended in the early 1990s, and oral histories of its residents. Edward Seidensticker's *Tokyo Rising: The City since the Great Earthquake* (New York: Alfred A. Knopf, 1990), and Paul Waley's *Tokyo Now and Then: An Explorer's Guide* (New York: Weatherhill, 1984), while they touch only briefly on San'ya, provide indispensable introductions to the Japanese capital's rich history.

A book-length study of Kamagasaki, Japan's largest *yoseba,* remains to be written in English. Tom Gill's *Men of Uncertainty: The Social Organization of Day Laborers in Contemporary Japan* (Albany: State University of New York Press, 2001), although focusing primarily on the Kotobuki *yoseba* in Yokohama, does offer trenchant accounts of every major day laborer quarter in Japan. *On the Margins of Japanese Society:*

Volunteers and the Welfare of the Urban Underclass (London: Routledge, 1997), by Carolyn Stevens, offers a positive view of Christian activism in the Kotobuki *yoseba* and thus a counterargument to Ōyama's rather severe take on Christian charity in chapter 5. Finally, Rey Ventura's *Underground in Japan* (London: Jonathan Cape, 1992) offers a view of the *yoseba* from a foreign (Filipino) perspective and thus another counterargument to Ōyama's scathing critique of the foreign migrant worker.

For a detailed study of the decades-long protests against the building and expansion of the Tokyo International Airport in Narita, mentioned by Ōyama in chapter 5, see David Apter and Nagayo Sawa, *Against the State: Politics and Social Protest in Japan* (Cambridge: Harvard University Press, 1984). For more on the *yakuza,* who have little control over the recruiting that goes on at the municipal employment agencies but a great deal of control over that which takes place on the street, see my *San'ya Blues;* see also *The Japanese Mafia: Yakuza, Law, and the State,* by Peter B. E. Hill (Oxford: Oxford University Press, 2003) and *Yakuza: Japan's Criminal Underworld,* expanded ed., by David E. Kaplan and Alec Dubro (Berkeley: University of California Press, 2003), for a description of, among other things, the link between *yakuza* gangs and construction companies in Japan. Those who share Ōyama's abiding love of sumo are invited to peruse Lora Sharnoff's *Grand Sumo: The Living Sport and Tradition* (Tokyo: Weatherhill, 1993) and Clyde Newton and Gerald J. Toff's *Dynamic Sumo* (Tokyo: Kodansha International, 2000), among other books, not to mention the many Web sites available on the sport.

Lastly, those interested in *Hōjōki,* the medieval essay, mentioned in the introduction, that some critics regard as a kind of inspiration for Ōyama's work, are encouraged to read one of the many translations available in English (for example, "An Account of My Hermitage," in Helen Craig McCullough, *Classical Japanese Prose: An Anthology* [Stanford: Stanford University Press, 1990], pp. 379–92).

English translations of haiku are available by the thousand; none that I know of, however, alludes to the lives of day laborers. That is unfortunate, as many fine haiku on this topic have in fact been published in both journals and books in Japanese. I take the liberty of quoting a haiku by Homma Takashi I know from memory, which is etched on a small stone tablet in a corner of a cozy San'ya shrine and presumably beyond the reach of copyright, in order to give readers an inkling of the subgenre's literary possibilities:

> *Tsuruhashi wo*   So quiet, so still
> *furaneba fuyuhi*   This bright winter day on which
> *shizuka nari*   I don't swing my pick